I0749185

QUEEN KURMANJAN OF THE MOUNTAINS

An Epic Poem

by Bubaisha Arstynbekova

English Language Edit
by Stephen M. Bland and Ola's Kool Kitchen,
Poetic Consultation given by Rev. Dr. David William Parry FRSA

London 2021

Printed in United Kingdom
Hertfordshire Press Ltd©2021
e-mail: publisher@hertfordshirepress.com
www.hertfordshirepress.com

QUEEN KURMANJAN OF THE MOUNTAINS

Bubaisha Arstynbekova ©

Translated from Kyrgyz by Zina Karaeva
Editor - Stephen M Bland, Timur Akhmedjanov
Poetic Consultation - Rev. Dr. David William Parry FRSA
Typeset - Alexandra Rey
cover image - Rahat Chukushova
Project manager - Angelina Krasnogir

British Library Catalogue in Publication Data
A catalogue record for this book is available from the British Library
Library of Congress in Publication Data
A catalogue record for this book has been requested

ISBN: 978-1-913356-32-3

ABOUT AUTHOR

Bubaisha Arstynbekova is the member of the Eurasian Creative Guild, winner of the Open Central Asia Book Forum and Literature Festival-2014, Honored Worker of the Culture of the Kyrgyz Republic, poet, public figure, and a member of the Kyrgyz National Writers' Union.

She is the member of the Public Council of the Ministry of Culture and the Chairwoman for the Information and Tourism of the Kyrgyz Republic from 2015-2017. Bubaisha Kuluevna was born on April 8th 1961, in the village of Toktogul, Zerger rural area of the Uzgen region, Osh oblast.

Bubaisha Arstynbekova's interest of the art of speech began during her school years, with her poems being published in periodicals. Since 1978, Bubaisha songs have become popular among the people, they were musicalized and she was known as a great poet. Her first collection of poems was called "For You" and it was published in 1999 by "Kyrgyzstan Basmasy". A review of the poems was written by the Kyrgyz national poet, Suerkul Turgunbaev, who wished her success and said: "I understood completely that she was given the gift to feel the unseen whisper of the poetic world and the artistic thinking of great human ability".

In 1999, the poetess Bubaisha Arstynbekova became a member of the National Writers' Union.

In 2008, the book "My Motherland is in my Eyesight - Karegimde Ata-Jurt" was published by the publishing house "Biyiktik". A review for this book was written by the Kyrgyz national poet, and national hero of the Kyrgyz Republic, Suyunbay Eraliev, who gave his blessings to her. The publication of the collection of poems "Karegimde Ata-Jurt" was especially and hotly debated in the creative sphere.

In 2008, a critic and famous writer of the Kyrgyz Republic, a doctor of philology and a professor, Beishebai Usubaliev, published his critical article in the newspaper "Jany-Ordo" and it was the subject of the great debate at that time. Beishebay Usubaliev wrote in his review that this book calls the young generation to be patriotic, to love their motherland and respect it. A people's poet of the Kyrgyz Republic and translator, Suslova, translated Bubaisha famous creation "Alai Queen ". Many works of art and documentaries have been written about the famous Kurmanjan Datka, known as the "Queen of Alai" - a remarkably great figure who played a huge role in the history of the Kyrgyz people as a united nation.

Bubaisha Arstynbekova's poem "Kurmanjan Datka" is not only a great contribution to the memory of that great woman for future generations, but it also explores the life and traditions of the Kyrgyz people, that accompanied the future Queen from her childhood to her last days before passing away. These are new perspectives about Kyrgyz customs and traditions that are being presented for the modern world.

These astonishing ethnographic finds, along with a natural description of the atmosphere in which the great Kurmanjan Datka grew up, matured and learned in, show the life of the great people's leader who respected and valued the traditions and ways of her ancestors. In addition, the poem "Kurmanjan Datka" written by Bubaisha Arstynbekova can be a useful material for studying the ethnographic field of national culture. Therefore, it can be recommended as a text book that could be used in the universities of the country. In particular, Beishebai Usubaliev, a scientist, doctor of philology, academician of the International Chyngyz Aitmatov Academy and a well-known writer, wrote in the "Ala-Too" magazine about Bubaisha poem "Kurmanjan Datka". He wrote that "if you read the descriptions of the traditions, you will want to look at it as a small part of a larger encyclopedia that reflects a bit on the Kyrgyz tradition, quite vividly. In this case, it is as if Bubaisha herself plays the role of the mother as well as the role of the writer, with it being impossible to separate them. When you read the whole poem, you can't help but be convinced that it was written by a poet - a mother or a mother-poet." Saying these words he blessed her.

In 2014, she took part in the Open Central Asia Book Forum & Literature Festival-2014, with her historical poem "Kurmanjan Datka", she won second place out of participates from over 20 countries, raising the flag of Kyrgyzstan up high.

Today, the historical poem "Kurmanjan Datka" has been translated into English and Russian, it found its readers at the global level and promotes Kyrgyz poetry all over the world. Bubaisha Arstynbekova is the writer of about a hundred musical songs. The song "Alymbek Datka" was composed by the people's artist of the Kyrgyz Republic, Sardarbek Jumaliev, and they were sung by people's artist of the Kyrgyz Republic, Salamat Sadykova. They are kept in the "Golden Fund", the Kyrgyz national television - radio cooperation. The Kyrgyz people's artists Aksuubai Atabaev, Ataibek Bodoshov, Kanykei Eralieva, honored worker of Culture of the Kyrgyz Republic, melodist Mamatibraim Bostonkulov, young melodists Alisher Tootaev, Suezdbek Iskenaliev, Bakyt Mamev, Jusupaaly Maseitov and many others. Salamat Sadykova, Elmira Kayip kyzy (deceased), Chyrmash Torobekov, Ilyaz Andash, Dinara Tilekeeva and other singers who have performed her songs.

QUEEN KURMANJAN OF THE MOUNTAINS

1.

Your eyes are bedazzled by the rays of the sun,
Your Ala-Too stretches high and wide.
The entire expanse is covered in a lush green carpet,
Looking like the paradise where you have always lived.

2.

The Kyrgyz of the highest Ala-Too,
Are as an arrow ready to shoot far ahead.
The traditions of antiquity, undying,
May fade, but never lose their lustre.

3.

Glaciers shine as mirrored surfaces,
Melting and merging into the mountain's rocky base.
I drank deeply and satiated my thirst, while
A golden spring cascades from the precipices.

4.

The land appears divine.
Its traditions as clear as the stars.
Crystal and luminous are each sunrise,
Like those observed at the dawn of time.

5.

Eagles sound among the high slopes, whereas
The Nightingale's aria can be heard through the trees;
Smooth as a woman's manicured hands,
One is stunned by nature's splendour.

6.

The arena emits a sunny glow.
One basks in the artistry of these landscapes.
Our hero, Manas, with the heart of a lion,
Embodies the greatness of our Kyrgyz nation.

7.

We are golden with a similarity to abundant jewels.
The wealth of Mother Earth combined with the coffers of state.
Hence, agents of the United Kingdom, China and Russia,
Wished to master our wonderland crossing the Great Silk Road.

8.

Thousands have travelled the Silk Road,
If you crave respect, open your hearts and welcome all.
If marauders should come with grievous intent,
They may take our lives, yet not our landscapes.

9.

We were ready to fall on the fields of battle,
But, our enemies were routed instead.
Truly, they saved their lands from invaders,
By uniting their forces to win at warfare.

10.

Ready to die for our nation,
We smote our enemies in battle,
We defended our country from every foe,
Joined by an all-encompassing duty.

11.

We never wearied of safeguarding our homes,
We were constantly prepared to shed blood for the state.
Everlastingly, recalling the fearlessness of the people,
Our ancestors preserved both honour and nation.

12.

Lion Manas maintained dominion over his kingdom and army.
Generous and modest, he oversaw this land.
Our women were wise, virtuous and traditional,
While Queen Kurmanjan reflected those values in herself.

13.

When ruminating on the life of Kurmanjan Datka,
My dark nights turned into white morns.
I considered her accomplishments and her life,
Her greatest endeavours as a guiding light for people.

BIRTH OF KURMANJAN

14.

In the sacred city of Osh, stands Sulayman Mountain,
Whereby a pristine river dashes like quicksilver:
Dazzling droplets from paradise fall, they say,
Feeding dark red berries and blackcurrants.

15.

In times of yore, there was a place called Orke,
Later it was changed to Japalak.
Eloquent, and of good disposition,
There lived Mamatbay and his wife Aikan, picture perfect.
She was a lady of clear conscience and uncommon decency,
Rich, while from royal blood. Mamatbay
Hailed from the Munduz tribe.
Considered philanthropic, he was deeply respected by his people.
Recorded in history as sincere and ethical,
His wife also considered Mamatbay handsome and benevolent.

16.

As a shepherd guards his flock,
This rich man bestowed mercy on the poor and slaves.
Altruistic and kind-natured,
His people showered him with well-earned blessings.

17.

As the days passed and the months flew by,
Aikan was desperate to be with child.
Praying to God to make her fruitful,
She additionally consulted shamans and doctors.

18.

Six years elapsed in barren misfortune,
But, they hoped that the seventh would bear good tidings.
'Please, don't forget to bring me blessings,'
Aikan often asked of Great God.

19.

They visited all the sacred places,
Longing for the scent of a newborn.
For seven long years, they hoped for a child,
Their hearts filled with anguish by the lengthy wait.

20.

There is a superstition saying to don the clothes
Of fecund women who have borne many children.
Gives blessings. This is how Aikan fulfilled her dream,
Following an elder's advice on how to conceive.

21.

Aikan's aunt-in-law's name was Umut,
She had born thirteen children.
The branches of her family were strong and blissful;
She even had two sets of twins.
Aikan intended to visit her mother-in-law, Ylpyhan,
And ask her to steal linen for the sake of a child.
For her trouble, she would bestow upon her a golden coin,
And a white kerchief to cover her head.

22.

Aikan went to her mother-in-law
Asking, 'Please, my dear, do me this service.
This superstition will save me'. She pleaded
And pleaded, doing her utmost to persuade her.

23.

Ylpyhan loved her darling Aikan,
Yet, found the task most onerous.
She was troubled by the theft asked of her.
Indeed, as she stole linen, it trailed along the ground.

24.

Suspecting Ylpyhan was in distress,
Umut asked her what the matter was?
Ylpyhan didn't know how to reply,
But, Aikan arrived at an opportune moment.

25.

'How are you, dear Aunty?' asked Aikan.
'Good, thank you,' replied Umut, asking that the table be laid.
When the two went into the kitchen for dishes,
Ylpyhan gave Aikan the purloined linen.

26.

'Please, do not tell anyone,' she asked, 'not even your beloved.'
So, when the table was set, Aikan was contented.
Indeed, she helped herself to roasted tealeaves with milk,
A special delicacy for guests.

27.

Having what she wanted, Aikan
Took great pleasure in their high tea.
Having what she needed,
She hid it under her arm.

28.

Heartened to see Aikan so happy,
Umut asked the reason for her surprise visit.
Thereafter, showering Aikan with benedictions, she said,
'Let God protect you and give you a child.'

29.

'My reason for coming,' Aikan replied,
'Was I dreamt that I cradled a baby at my breast.
Let God bless us all, Aunty Umut,
I wish to have twins like yours.'

30.

'May all your dreams come true,' said Umut.
'Do you know the old wives tale about wearing a linen
That belonged to a fertile woman? Ask God seven times your
Wish, and surely He will grant it.'

31.

With the stolen linen,
Aikan hurried home.
Certainly, she wore the linen every day without fail,
Looking forward to becoming pregnant.

32.

The couple found a horse to sacrifice
To please God enough to grant them a child.
Well-wishers abounded at their feast,
Bestowing upon them felicitations.

33.

Grateful to all their friends and relatives,
Aikan prayed she should not be barren.
Pining for a child of her own
She beseeched God to let her be fruitful.

34.

One night, there was an omen.
In the twilight between waking and sleeping,
Mamatbay saw a bird of prey in a hypnagogic hallucination.
Its wings strong and looming large, it circled a great mountain.

35.

With a supper of meat clutched between its claws,
It swooped and glided endlessly;
A clear harbinger of abundance
Through the vision of this strange dream.

36.

Forged from silver and gold,
A tomahawk was in his Mamatbay's clasp,
Like a pure silk of rainbow colours,
The bird flew down and sat on his hand.

37.

His arms couldn't hold the immense feathered beast,
His shoulders burned as though aflame.
The fowl displayed the strength of an eagle,
Although put forward its head to be petted.

38.

When dawn broke. He undertook his ablutions
Without revealing his vision.
He prayed to God, who was moved by his entreaties
On the slopes of the hallowed Sulayman Mountain.

39.

He told no one about his vision,
Even Aikan wasn't privy to it.
I will only reveal the details, he thought,
At the celebration of the child's birth.

40.

As he climbed holy Sulayman Mountain,
Pondering his dream and its meaning,
He divined he'd have a son who would lead the nation,
As powerful as the bird in his augury.

41.

Content with the Creator,
Mamatbay gladly returned home.
An aurora blossomed forth across the sky,
As Aikan brewed their tea.

42.

His face radiant with happiness,
Mamatbay's eyes shone with gratification.
Beaming, whilst reflecting on his trance,
He was satiated by prophecies.

43.

Sensing that he was keeping something from her,
Aikan asked, 'Darling, what is it?'
Looking at her with an enigmatic smile,
'Everything's fine,' he said, imagining her pregnancy.

44.

Mamatbay's prescience came to pass,
In time, Aikan became pregnant.
Still, eagerly awaiting their child,
He planned a tremendous celebratory feast.

45.

With the passage of time, snowdrops appeared,
It was the year 1811.
The birth pangs began and Aikan was in agony
As the snows of old winter melted.

46.

A missive was sent to the godmother, Janyl,
In order to prepare for the birth of the child.
A faithful gem of the people,
She was to be the midwife and deliver the baby.

47.

It was a great distance for Janyl to travel,
But, she arrived in time to oversee the birth.
Thence, as she said prayers and readied the waters,
Aikan's face was red and her lips clenched.

48.

'God, you blessed me with the boon of pregnancy,
Please, help me give birth!' Aikan cried.
Clutching her quilt with white knuckles, she said,
'Let your path always be righteous.'

49.

Sadly, Aikan suffered great torments in labour,
Both Janyl and neighbours begging help from Creations All.
Soon, though, the child's cry was heard,
And free from danger, the birth was a success.

50.

In Japalak, spring was in the air.
Thus, during the festival of Kurman Ait.
On the very day when the newborn appeared,
Their village glistened like a sunbeam.

51.

A marvellous daughter was born in the village,
Such a beautiful wonder.
The godmother in rapture with the baby's face,
Bonded with the child as it cried.

52.

Throughout the day white rays of light appeared,
Like an augur of meaning unknown.
So, fearing they were an omen of sacrifice,
Aikan's heart was aflutter with angst.

53.

'Oh Mamatbay, congratulations,
Your daughter has arrived, glad tidings to you,'
Mamatbay heard time and again, but recalled his premonition.
Of seeing an eagle in a dream, but a daughter?
'Dear God, I'm overjoyed,' he whispered,
Even though he couldn't forget his dream.

54.

They received gold, silver and other gifts,
Albeit Aikan felt different now the child was born.
She will be a cherished girl and an astute woman,
She suddenly sensed whilst lying exhausted.

55.

When Aikan held her child for the first time,
To suckle her and truly observe her properly,
She noticed shining rays, which blinded her.
It was like holding the lightning.

56.

'Did I create a girl or a star?' she asked,
As the light from the child overpowered her.
She passed the child to her godmother,
Who took the extraordinary bairn in her arms.

57.

Janyl looked at Aikan and said,
'My dear, take the nipper into your own hands.'
Since Aikan was still astonished upon seeing her,
Anyway, as she put the baby to her breast to suckle.
A heat rapidly arose from the babe
Like a blazing fire.
May she be happy and God protect her, she thought,
Genuinely, a remarkable child.

58.

Mamatbay melted like snow. He was delighted.
His paternal feelings continuing to grow.
Still, the eagle of his dream
Had turned out to be a swan;
The gold, silver and pure silk of his vision
In reality proved to be a girl.

59.

During Passover, Mamatbay
Was chosen to be an adjudicator;
Dividing food and provisions evenly,
Clearly, he ensured each household's share was uniform.

60.

Let God make my child fortunate and wealthy,
Let her birth be auspicious for all of us, he thought.
And because she was born on a holy day,
Let her name be Kurmanjan.

BY MELTED BUTTER

61.

Aikan kept melted butter
To place on the baby's lips.
It's a tradition of our ancestors from time immemorial,
Set to ensure an infant's future affluence.

62.

So, Aikan saved this butter,
By placing it in a dried sheep's stomach.
She knew all the rituals of her native land,
Her mother had taught her everything.

63.

Aikan's mother came to the baby's gala,
When all the matriarchs gathered together.
Thence, placing butter around the little one's mouth,
They performed this significant observance.

64.

Aikan's mother, Umai,
Daubed the melted butter in the baby's mouth.
'Let the butter that is spread,' she said,
'Make her prosperous and content.'

65.

Mother Eve, protector of women and children,
Visit this baby in person.
'Let the infants words be like butter melting slowly;
Let her life be laced with honey,' she said.

66.

'Let there always be butter;
Let her be important like a queen.
Let her storage be always full of wheat,
Let people have all the food they need.'

67.

‘Spreading melted butter in the baby’s mouth
Signifies that her life will be smooth.
Let her become exceptional,
Like an elegantly designed tapestry.’

68.

‘Let there always be butter at home,
Let her be polite and prudent.
Let her be someone who takes care of her parents;
Let even the serpent bow its head to her wisdom.
Let friends and enemies alike,
Admire her for her eloquence.’

69.

‘Let the child be blessed,
Let her never speak ill.
Let her words be harmonious,
Let her life be like butter,
Let her days be succulent.’

70.

‘Let there always be butter.
Let her wear a girl’s cap.
Let her character be compassionate and composed,
Let her be fortuitous in everything.
Let her be discerning for all of her days.’

71.

'Let there always be butter.
May her life be long.
Let her become a public speaker,
And an advocate for the people.'

72.

'Let the words she articulates be both
Advantageous and persuasive.
Let them always be buttery,
Let her nature be jubilant and triumphant.'

THE BIRTH FEAST

73.

Motivated by these festivities,
Their neighbours came to see the babe,
So, celebrating Kurman Ait and the birth,
The atmosphere was more than cordial.
Certainly, a sense of glee was in the air,
Like the scent of this newborn for which they had waited.

74.

Many congratulations were offered;
Gaiety abounded!
May Kurmanjan have a long and prosperous life,
Was the single thought
Which united them all.

THE CRADLE FEAST

75.

After these events had passed,
Came the rite of Kurmanjan's cradle.
As such, the child's grandmother enjoyed this the most,
By presenting a red cedar crib with the fragrance of juniper.

76.

Everybody praised this distinctive crib.
They asked who had made the embroidery,
As friends and relatives commented,
'Let this cradle be tickled pink by our babe.'
Further, Mamatbay was pleased with his in-laws,
Who had brought a foal to the jamboree.

77.

With her deepest desire having been fulfilled,
Aikan prepared to sing a lullaby.
Desiring the best for her infant,
She was happy to follow this old Kyrgyz custom.

78.

Let God grant wisdom and humanity,
To the invocations of every mother's song.
It is a proud observance to sing this lullaby,
Willing longevity, thereby, and nurslings' well-being.

79.

With Aikan's longing a reality,
She sang her words with relish,
Stating her hopes and aspirations,
She gently rocked the cradle.

THE SONG OF THE CRADLE FEAST

80.

'Let your cradle be golden,
Let your cradle be bright.
Let my baby sleep soundly.
Let a cradle gala be for my child.'

81.

'Let your cradle be made of silver,
Let your cradle be bright.
Let me rock you to sleep, sweet one,
Let a cradle gala be for my child.'

82.

'Please, burn cedar leaves
To remove negativity.
From anyone with evil intentions,
Please, burn anise,
Abolishing any ill-will,
Directed at my baby's soul.'

83.

'We beseech you, Mother Eve,
To protect this child from the evil eye,
And drop into Kurmanjan's cradle
A spread of boorsoq, candy and butter.'

THE LULLABY

84.

'Sleep, my child and peace be with you,
All through the darkest hours.
God will send angels to guard over you
Throughout the night.'

85.

'My dearest girl, let rest be with you,
Sleep my child, don't cry.
Be good for your Mother,
Until Father returns from the mountains.'

86.

'When Father arrives, Mother will wake you,
And then my honey-child,
Daddy will play with you,
Until night falls again.'

87.

'O, my baby, O, my baby,
Please rest in your cradle.
Let your life be long,
And your spirit be harmonious.'

88.

‘O, my child of the moon,
May you be insightful.
May even strangers be dazzled,
By the wisdom of your soul.’

89.

‘O, my beautiful girl,
With a spirit as flawless as a pearl;
Let everyone rejoice,
To hear your name is Kurmanjan.’

90.

‘O, my darling girl,
May you be as pure as cotton;
Let the people be overjoyed,
At the mention of your name.’

91.

‘Sleep, my child, may peace attend you.
Be a great boon for our nation.
May you be treasured, my honey,
And invaluable to your people.’

92.

'O, my darling child,
Your cradle is made of cedar.
Let your land be affluent:
Let the people eat heartily.'

93.

'O, my moon-girl,
Be of value to your homeland.
Be a leader among forty girls,
Be a candle in the dark.'

94.

'O, my deer-girl,
Let you be my life's inspiration.
Let you be the silver of my house,
Be the nightingale of your people.'

95.

'O, my beloved,
Let your hair be finely styled
And beautifully adorned.
May you live like a Khan,
And always be optimistic.'

96.

‘O, my dearest,
Let your hair be as long as a river
With plaits like forty streams.
May you spend your days with Royalty,
Let your life be filled with Khans.’

97.

‘O, my darling,
In the cradle, you will sleep.
And when you awake I’ll allow you
To scatter my beads through the house and yard.’

98.

‘And when your Mother asks
Why you did it, my darling, please know,
That your Mother will still be grateful,
That you scattered her beads.’

99.

‘O, my sweet thing,
Asleep in your lovely cradle.
Know that you can spread and scatter
Whatever’s in your Father’s barn.’

100.

'When the wheat is gathered in the fall,
Let Father enjoy playtime with you.
Know that his heart is lightened,
When you sit near him, my honey-child.'

101.

'O, my lovely girl,
May you be a first-rate seamstress.
Renowned all over the globe;
As revered as any boy in the land.'

102.

'O, my dear honey,
May you live a limitless life.
Let your home be a palace;
Your husband, a king with a castle,
May he look after you well.'

103.

'O, my honey-child,
Let your home be a mansion.
Let there be great prosperity in your life,
May your spouse be a grand Emperor.'

THE CEREMONY DEDICATED TO THE INFANT'S FIRST STEPS.

Cutting the rope is a Kyrgyz tradition. When a child attempts to walk for the first time, family and friends gather to commemorate this event. Everyone is invited to participate in a race to cut the rope that had been tied around the toddler's legs. The first to reach the finish line cuts the thread, receiving a prize and great distinction. Everyone else receives consolation prizes, and afterwards, they enjoy a huge feast. This event traditionally comes with the benediction: 'Let the child inherit the velocity of the winner of the race.'

104.

May this child never stumble on the road of life.
May their fortune always be promising.
It's a parent's duty to observe the cutting of the knot,
And make of it a sumptuous affair.

105.

Mamatbay followed the unwritten laws of his ancestors,
And made an occasion out of the cutting of the rope.
All ages engaged in the contest, though
Some couldn't manage the entire distance.
Clearly, they were upset that they couldn't cut the rope,
Some cried and others fell,
Disappointed that they couldn't complete the course.

106.

Notwithstanding all the hullabaloo,
Kurmanjan took her first steps timidly, but with exhilaration.
What an adorable sprite the Kyrgyz people had!
Hence, Aikan laid out a spread of confectionaries,
So there were prizes for all
And no one left empty-handed.

107.

Mamatbay distributed cattle and cash as awards;
While Kurmanjan had gifted them with her first stroll.
She looked ahead with confidence,
As a parent's dream come true.

108.

With good wishes from all the people,
Her parents were exultant,
And took relish at standing by her side.
Beseeching God's everlasting grace for her.
Her grandpa then took her hands,
Saying, 'Tai, tai, my dear, come take your first steps.'

THE SPEECH COMMEMORATING HER FIRST PEREGRINATIONS

109.

'Tai, tai, come, take your first steps.
Go to your dear Grandma.
Take your first steps, my angel,
And Grandpa will present you with a gift.
You will ride a horse, my dear.'

110.

'Tai, tai, come, take your first steps.
Come to Grandpa.
Toddle over and leave your first footprints,
Grandpa has a pony for you.
You will ride a horse, my lovely.'

111.

'Tai, tai, tai, come, take your first steps.
Tai, tai, tai, honey-child.
Start your path of good fortune.
Forge ahead, my sweet, do not stumble,
My beloved, sweet pea.'

112.

'Tai, tai, come, take your first steps.
Head towards your future
Without encountering obstacles.
Be tolerant, my little beauty,
You must take your first steps.'

113.

'Tai, tai, come, take your first steps.
Let your strides be happy.
Let your Father bless you,
Let your Mother bless you,
May your life's journey be joyous.'

114.

'Tai, tai, come, take your first steps.
Let your life be as long as a river;
Let your valley be filled with cattle.
May you always be merry,
May you always be thoughtful and mighty.'

KURMANJAN'S CHILDHOOD AND SIGNS OF HER MAJESTY

115.

A budding angel was in the village,
Nearby the sanctified Sulayman Mountain.
Who could have foretold that Kurmanjan,
Was destined to be a great leader of her land?

116.

Her godmother, Janyl,
Was close to beloved Kurmanjan.
Doting, she was present for all of the major events
In the young girl's life.
She tended to her and protected her from the evil eye,
By visiting Kurmanjan often.

117.

Once, she came with a buttered loaf.
Kurmanjan was ten and an amusing little girl,
Who greeted Janyl with respect and endearment.
Her godmother remarked to Aikan,
'Your daughter is exceptional, isn't she?'
Aikan replied courteously, but this fact she already knew.

118.

'They informed me about Kurmanjan's abilities;
When she was born, shining rays
Poured from the heavens,' said Janyl.
'Did you not find that peculiar?'

119.

'I recall that glittering irradiation.
She is unique and it causes her difficulties.
I believe she can predict the future,' said Aikan,
'I believe she has a sixth sense.'

120.

'She is young and doesn't understand her gifts,
Though I've observed she's a proficient fortune teller.
Everyone can tell she's extraordinary,
Let God protect her from the evil eye.'

121.

'She is a little imp, my darling.
Raised without constraints, yet mild-mannered.
She is eloquent and outgoing,
At times, I feel overwhelmed by her talents.'

122.

‘She is determined and grasps opportunities;
If need be, she is aggressive like a boy.
Her family all know it,
She is strong, yet possesses a delicate soul.’

123.

‘She can ride a horse with nimble grace,
And is an eloquent public speaker.
She inherited her father’s jolly disposition,
And is voracious at all times.’

124.

‘I wouldn’t say she’s mischievous,
But she tells things as they are.
She’s affectionate, informed and puckish;
A brilliant little jewel in our family,
For which I’m grateful to God.’

125.

‘Even with her friends,
When they take to bickering between themselves,
She is a real leader amongst them,
By directing them to stop arguing.
And they obediently follow her advice.
Sometimes I admonish her that she shouldn’t command them so.’

126.

'Occasionally, she wakes from a dream,
Bolt upright, frightened at what she has seen.
A prophecy of future events;
She had the power of divination,
Soothsaying without even trying.'

127.

'Kurmanjan predicted that her father would go to Kok Bory,
And there, unexpected misfortune would befall him.
Kurmanjan saw beforehand,
That her father's leg would be broken.'

128.

'"Oh Mother," she told me, "I had a bad dream.
I saw my father carousing with a horse.
He tried to lift a goat as large as a calf,
Then I saw a man with broken bones."'

129.

'"Father was a mess, crying out,
His horse's saddle was broken,
His right boot fell upon the ground,
His foot wasn't right on the stirrup.
He fell hard on the stony ground,
The collar of his coat was ripped."'

130.

'Praying to God, I touched my collar,
"Dreams aren't real," I told her.
"Let's hurry in the direction of Ak-Buura,
Let's tell your dream to the river."'

131.

There was a refreshing breeze on the riverbank,
The water was pristine.
Let Ak-Buura wash away this bad dream,
Aikan prayed for a long time.
Repeated her mother's words,
Kurmanjan also asked for God's help,
Turning her face to the heavens.

132.

Best to forget this dream, Aikan thought,
The river will wash it away.
God will keep her safe,
And cleanse her with these waters.
Kurmanjan, though, suspected she was enchanted:
Felt something dangerous within herself.

133.

Mamatbay paid no mind to the dream,
Believing it merely an overactive imagination.
He left for the Ulak Tartysh* contest,
Though everyone felt uneasy and asked him not to.

134.

Overall, she begged to go with him,
But, Mamatbay didn't take his beloved daughter.
He tricked her into thinking he wasn't leaving,
And on finding him gone, she dashed to her mother.

135.

'Oh Mother, you know my dream,
I prayed to God to save my father.
I appealed to God to keep daddy safe,'
Sobbed the troubled Kurmanjan.

136.

'Don't cry, my darling,
Your father's at the feast,'
Aikan consoled her daughter.
'I know, dearest mother,' Kurmanjan said,
'Yet, I don't know how I can help him.'

**(Ulak Tartysh, also known as Buzkashi is the Kyrgyz national sport. It is like a mix between polo and rugby, except a goat's carcass is used instead of a ball.)*

137.

'Don't court trouble if it hasn't found you,'
Counselled Aikan, 'Don't cry over dreams.
Your father is in the village of Olokon,
For the Buzkashi tournament.

138.

'Don't be upset, don't be glum,
Don't fret over your dream.
Your father is in the village of Olokon.
He will soon return bearing gifts.'

139.

'O, Mother, this is serious,' sobbed Kurmanjan,
'I saw his leg maimed.'
'Don't say so, honey,' pleaded Aikan,
'Away, away with these words!
Let us believe he will come home unharmed,
And that God will always protect him.'

140.

Aikan embraced her daughter once more,
And pressed her to her breast,
Singing such a sweet lullaby
That Kurmanjan was shortly asleep.

141.

When Kurmanjan awoke at noon,
She immediately inquired,
'Where is Father? Has he come home?'
But, Aikan just said he'd return soon.

142.

'Your father is an excellent horseman,' she said,
'And is fond of Ulak Tartysh.
He's keen to participate in the contest,
It is a highlight of the season.'

143.

Aikan was doing household chores,
While they discussed the national game,
When they spotted Mamatbay slung over his horse,
Arriving at their homestead.

144.

Kurmanjan was annoyed at her father,
And recalled the details of her nightmare.
'O, Daddy, you didn't listen to my prediction,
And look what happened to you, dear Papa,'
She sobbed as she clasped his chest.

145.

‘My leg may be broken, but do not fret,
God saved me,’ said Mamatbay.
‘The healer bandaged my wounds,
And I hardly feel any pain.’

146.

Saying more soothing words,
He tousled his daughter’s hair.
Mamatbay soon fell asleep,
But, Kurmanjan didn’t move.

147.

After the prophecy had come to pass,
Kurmanjan knew there was a lion in her soul.
She whispered slowly to her mother,
‘This Red Lion will always protect me.’

148.

‘Of what do you speak; is it your dream?’
Aikan asked her daughter.
‘It’s more than a dream; it’s something within me,’
Said Kurmanjan; ‘It doesn’t frighten me anymore.’

149.

'Don't tell anyone else,
Keep it to yourself,' said Aikan;
And though she wasn't convinced it was true,
Her daughter's words unsettled her.

150.

Awaking, Mamatbay pressed her to his chest,
'What is this Red Lion you speak of?' he asked.
'It's something that lives within me,' she answered;
'When you fell from the horse, this lion helped you.'

151.

Concentrating on these words,
He looked at his wife in bewilderment.
Aikan explained as she fixed Kurmanjan's hair
That their daughter had a guardian spirit watching over her.

152.

Her father kissed Kurmanjan's face and said,
'If you have a unique ability, let it be so.
You are the only star in my sky,
And I wish you nothing but happiness.'

KURMANJAN'S ADOLESCENT YEARS

153.

Time flew like a bird in the sky,
The name of Kurmanjan became renowned across the land.
She was uncommon amongst her peers;
Admired for her knowledge and wit.

154.

She was a stunning vision to behold,
Great attention was lavished upon her.
She was a morning star in the dawn,
Her parent's house set aglow by her presence.

155.

Like a flower, her blossom unfurled every day,
She was as slender as a birch tree.
Her eyes twinkled like celestial bodies,
Or, as a full moon on a caliginous evening.

156.

Her eyes were dark as blackcurrants,
And her breasts as sweet as apples.
She dreamt of her future constantly,
Wishing for good fortune.

157.

Her lips were red as poppies,
That grew on the Kerme-Too Mountains.
Where people had lived since time immemorial;
Completely fulfilled by their surroundings.

158.

There is a sweet fragrance in the jailoo,
Where the nightingales sing and trill.
The snow upon high peaks
Dazzled everything in the sun.

159.

Her hair was long and flowing,
Her laughter flawless as birdsong.
Her neck was slender like a swan;
Her thin hips charming as daylight.

160.

In Japalak, the grapes are as sweet as nectar,
And tender young Kurmanjan,
Like a highland flower,
Hailed from this bewitching place.

161.

As pretty as a picture,
And as fresh as the waters of Ak-Buura,
Her slender figure drew attention,
With young men extolling her pulchritude,
Kurmanjan became a woman.

162.

She grew up quickly, and many men wanted to marry her.
Since childhood, however,
Kurmanjan had been promised to Torokul's son.
It is taboo to break such a commitment in our culture,
So, no one dared to ask for her hand.

163.

It was normal for women to marry young,
And to heed their parent's advice on this matter.
Kurmanjan was seventeen-years-old,
She must soon start a family of her own,
And who one would marry was a matter of destiny.

164.

So, Kurmanjan agreed to her fate,
For there was no other she loved.
It caused her great consternation,
That no one had truly
Captured her heart.

165.

Aikan spoke frequently to her daughter,
And reminded her of the match.
Kurmanjan countered
That she didn't love Kulseit,
But, much to her vexation
There was no man in the village that she wanted to marry.

166.

'Nobody meets your expectations here,' said Aikan,
'You will not find anyone good enough, my dear.
This match was made when you were born,
You can't break this engagement, no one will support you.'

167.

'I don't know how to behave,' said Kurmanjan,
'My thoughts on this matter cause me tremendous agony,
I would like to marry someone,
Who I feel is an equal partner.'

168.

'Oh, my daughter, you are seventeen now,
Your words are but a pipe dream.
At eighteen, folks will say you're an old lady,
Then you won't be able to find a suitable young man.'

169.

'No, Mother,' said Kurmanjan, 'you're wrong,
This is not mere fancy; it's forecast in my destiny.
If I marry Torokul's son, Kulseit today,
Tomorrow, I will be separated.'

170.

'No, don't say this; it's a bad omen.
You must believe in a positive outcome.
Don't say such things before your wedding,
You'll be happily married to Kulseit, my beloved.'

171.

Both parents discharged their instructions to Kurmanjan,
Though disconcerted by her objections.
For although Kurmanjan and Kulseit had both
Grown up in the valleys and pastures,
She didn't love him and she wept.

172.

Kurmanjan could see no way out,
So, she consented to the marriage.
She did not want to shame her parents,
So, acquiesced to their command.

173.

Torokul was a judge and head of the Joosh tribe,
Whilst Mamatbay was a shepherd.
According to custom, he'd approached Mamatbay,
Requesting his daughter's hand for his son.

174.

Kurmanjan believed it was her fate
To meet a man she truly loved.
It was something she'd dreamt of her entire life,
And kept very close to her heart.

175.

Her mood disagreeable,
Kurmanjan, tortured by heartache
By not finding her true love,
Felt pangs akin to grief.

176.

Crushed and dolorous, with no cause for hope,
Kurmanjan could find no solace.
There was nothing to do but acquiesce;
No one was interested in her inner life,
No one seemed to care what she thought.

177.

Torokul came to finalise the match.
Arriving with camels and horses.
He bestowed many golden objects on Mamatbay,
Who custom dictated must host the wedding.

178.

Kurmanjan was disgruntled with her fiancé,
Yet, there was nothing she could do,
Since they had been engaged from childhood,
So, she determined to explore her fortune with Kulseit.

179.

The wedding feast lasted for seven days:
Relatives and villagers coming together,
The dowry was forty camels.
Kurmanjan rode with her husband
On her father's stallion.
It was their wedding gift to her,
They wanted their daughter to be happy.

KURMANJAN'S LAMENT BEFORE THE WEDDING

180.

Kurmanjan had a heavy heart;
She wanted to like living with Kulseit,
But, he was strange and peculiar,
She could never be close to him.

181.

'I couldn't fly over the horizon, like Aichurok,
Wearing my swan dress with wings.
I couldn't find my true love
On the banks of the Ak-Buura River.'

182.

'I couldn't fly through the firmaments, like Aichurok,
I couldn't fly over the Kerme-Too.
No one understands my desire,
I couldn't find my true love nearby.'

183.

'My expectations were dashed,' she sang softly,
'And I couldn't reach for the mountains.
How long will I continue to suffer,
Without finding my true love?'

184.

'I'm agitated and my nerves are so fraught
That I cannot live in the sun.
How long will I be unhappy,
Without finding my true love?'

185.

'If only I could soar
To the peaks;
I want to fly higher still,
In search for my true love.'

186.

'If your heart is in the fire,
It will turn to cinders,
But, if your spouse is the right one,
You can rise above the flames.'

187.

'Albeit my heart is consumed by fire,
And these ashes will be blown away.
If only I could have found true love,
I would surely learn to fly.'

KURMANJAN'S SPEECH BEFORE LEAVING HER HUSBAND

188.

'There are birch trees and walls in the yard,
Kulseit is my husband.
He doesn't value my needs;
He doesn't understand the simplest thing.'

189.

'The birch trees are ablaze,
I am sickened by my husband.
He shows me no respect;
He is such a fool.'

190.

'Picking a rich harvest of wheat,
My father-in-law is a very rich man.
My husband, though, is an aberrant oddball,
I have never seen such a man.'

191.

'My mother-in-law is truly a lady,
Greatly esteemed throughout the nation.
I do not know how they had such a son,
He is not a person I can love.'

192.

'I can't bear such suffering,
Each moment is excruciating.
At night, I will sneak away from him;
I will be forever free.'

193.

'It's my ambition to be liberated,
Though I'm expecting obstacles.
I will look forward to my future paradise,
I'll dare to live a desirable life.'

194.

'This will be a difficult time:
There is no divorce in my culture.
I will surely be punished
As a runaway bride.
They might even kill me.
But, I'm ready to die if need be.'

195.

'I will never love Kulseit;
He does not treat me as an equal.
Yet, I will meet my sweetheart one day,
I am certain it will come to pass.'

KURMANJAN'S FLIGHT FROM HER HUSBAND

196.

Months passed, Kurmanjan grew disappointed,
Deliberating on how she could find love.
A moment with the right man, she thought,
Is better than a lifetime with the wrong one.
After leaving Kulseit, she decided
To return to her parent's house in the country.

197.

It was midnight when she fled,
Riding her horse most rapidly
To avoid Kulseit's soldiers,
Who would have forced her back.

198.

The river was overflowing when she reached it,
Nevertheless, it was better to die
Than to return to Kulseit,
And so, she entered the white waters.

199.

'If God will see me through,' she thought,
'I'll be overjoyed to see my parents one last time,
But, if I am destined to die,
Death is better than to return to him.'

200.

'O, God, how can I survive?
How can I cross this river of misfortune?'
She wept, feeling alone in the world.
'Will my father be able to find my bones?'

201.

'Sink or swim, I accept my fate,
I give myself over to God's will.
If it's not pre-destined for me to reach Japalak,
I'm ready to meet my Maker,'
She said as she entered the river.

202.

While she prayed to God for safe passage,
And to avoid a watery grave,
A wave lowered the water level,
And something soft met her hand.

203.

Was it God's hand that saved her?
Something unseen held her passage firm.
Something magical and mysterious,
Delivered her to the far shore.

204.

When she realised she was unharmed,
She knelt upon the riverbank,
Praising God and giving thanks,
Whereafter she saw a Red Lion watching her.

205.

Overwhelmed by possible danger,
She offered up invocations,
Lauding God as she knelt,
She was grateful for her life.

206.

She continued her journey through the fields,
Ruminating upon her prospects.
She couldn't believe she'd managed to escape,
And forged ahead deep in prayer.

207.

'God,' she whispered, 'I'm profoundly content.
I'm beholden to you,
For you heard my call,
And sent a sacRed Lion to save my life.'

208.

As she spoke these words,
Ahead, she saw five ravenous lions
Afront the darkened forest.
'Time for me to meet my true death,' she thought,
But, there was no other way to go forward
Into the dismal forest.

209.

Kurmanjan was terrified
That her body would never be found,
That the remains of her flesh,
Would prove to be victuals for vultures.
Still, edging forward soaked in sweat,
She braved the lions in her path.

210.

Quivering, she beseeched God,
As she drew close upon the beasts.
Yet, they simply stared as she passed them,
Although they could have killed her with a single bite.

211.

Scarcely able to believe her good fortune,
That the savage lions let her be, she proclaimed,
'I accept you as my protector, my Red Lion!
You are the only one I truly believe in,'
She affirmed nearing her parent's home.

212.

The Red Lion was always with her,
So, she endearingly named it, 'my valiant Leo,'
Acknowledging it as her one true guardian,
And accepting all of its aspects and traits.

213.

'Among juniper bushes and birches,
In untamed woods or on the highest peaks,
May my father find me,'
She whispered to herself whilst travelling.
Albeit, her mind remained melancholy with thoughts
Of what Kulseit's soldiers would do if they captured her.

214.

She eagerly anticipated reuniting with her parents,
Memories being by her father's side aflooding
For hunting trips and for fowling,
As she fell into a deep slumber.

215.

O, how sweet her childhood had been,
Visiting neighbours and playing,
Wearing her newly-sown smock,
And her brightly embroidered bonnet.

216.

How she'd treasured each morning
The aroma of Mother's freshly baked bread,
And the hot tea with cream which would be at hand,
As she'd awaken her lovingly and kiss her forehead.

217.

She'd enjoyed being half awake,
And refusing to be roused by her Mother's kisses;
Yet, it was as if a century had passed since then:
A century of pining.

218.

In her dream, she remembered how
She would chase after her father, saying,
'My beloved Papa, I will accompany you everywhere.'
'Some places are forbidden for girls,'
He'd admonished, but she'd insisted,
Following him even to Ulak Tartysh.

219.

In the remarkable sport of Buzkashi,
Participants are pleased if they acquire a carcass.
Clearly, the person who wins the goat's cadaver,
Will also win praise from the other competitors.

220.

'O, Mamatbay please give me the goat!'
'Let your daughter be happy, please, pass me the goat.'
'May you soon have a son, please, pass me the goat,'
Everyone shouted after trailing him.
As the violent dust of the game settled,
It was an amazing sight to see.

221.

It is a competition handed down by our forebears,
Hounding after the goat's carcass on horseback,
Hastening to take it from each other,
Whilst battling onwards through exhaustion.

222.

Kurmanjan vividly dreamt of these scenes
Despite the beastly fright she had suffered.
Shortly, though, she was awoken,
Since a man's voice unsettled her.

223.

Was this man a trapper
Craving deer and wild sheep?
Who is he with the booming voice?
Is he merely part of a larger party?

224.

It was a rocky and arduous passage:
Reaching this place for men and women alike.
'Who is that man?' she wondered,
Both dazzled by his potent tone
And made uneasy by his presence.

225.

She saw him on a white horse with a silver bridle,
His demeanour both tolerant, yet also ferocious.
He resembled a lion to her,
With his straight nose and luminous eyes.

226.

'Who are you?' he asked of her.
Kurmanjan looked at him thoughtfully.
First, a lion had helped her cross the river,
Then, five lions had allowed her safe transit;
Now, she hoped her benefactor was also a lion.

227.

Kurmanjan reasoned further,
Her champion was a lion,
And here is a man with a leonine aspect.
Yet, the rider was about to dismount,
So, Kurmanjan stopped him, saying,
'Don't be in a hurry to get off your horse,
Don't be surprised, and please listen to my words.'

228.

In Osh, not far from Kerme-Too is the village of Japalak,
Where the immaculate Ak-Buura flows.
According to custom, I am called Kurmanjan,
And I was born in Japalak.

229.

'My grandfather was Mungushbay,
My father's name is Mamatbay, I am his only daughter.
I was married to a man who was unsuitable,
I loathed him, so I ran away
To escape my suffering.'

230.

'Your name is most elegant,' he replied,
'I will treasure the words you have spoken forever.
I am Alymbek, son of Asanbiy,
Of the Bargy tribe from the Alay area.'

231.

'My family and I hold the noble titles of Datka,
We were hunting and fowling, but I stopped to rest.'
Still, searching for the right reply,
Kurmanjan thought deeply.
'Fortune is not forged by our hands,
Even you can't exchange one fate for another,'
She said whilst gazing at him transfixed.

232.

Travellers shall cross each other's paths,
But, their ways of life and fortunes may differ,
Alymbek reflected, albeit saddened by the thought of
Her taking his whip, as in a game of Kyz kuu.

233.

Not knowing what to do,
Kurmanjan said, 'I am not jealous
Of you or of your family;
I wish you nothing but good health and happiness.'

234.

'I appreciate your generosity,' said Alymbek,
And as he beheld her, he was smitten.
Wistful, he wished they could remain conjoined,
For she would make a wonderful wife,
Supporting him through difficult times:
A better half and life partner.

235.

If she took his whip, he wondered,
Would it be an ill-fated portent for the land?
Indeed, as Alymbek scrutinised her,
His thoughts were in disarray.

236.

His reflections flew like a white falcon
Through an uncommon sky.
He recognised Kurmanjan was astute and quick-witted,
And spoke to her very respectfully.

237.

'I have a question for you, my dear lady,
When flowers entwine, they flourish.
If a lion encounters a woman with a guardian lion,
What will this lioness do?'

238.

'Only if flowers suit each other well,' she replied.
'It's of great fortune for the florid couple.
What a pity the lion who found this woman
With her sentinel beast is not a bachelor!'

239.

'What a marvellous answer,
You certainly solved my riddle.
Yet, have you a question for me?
It is your turn to ask whatever you choose.'

240.

'A person from a fine clan,' she said,
'Surely has no interest in meeting a strange lady.
Who had no esteem for her abandoned husband,
Who dared break from tradition and her marriage vow?'

241.

'If you left your husband, breaking with custom,
That is a true test of fate;
But, if golden coins are covered with dust,
They are still seen as gold, not dust.'

242.

'I'm delighted to hear your warmhearted words,
Whilst you would equate me to gold;
But, I've already given you my response,
And regret you belong to another.'

243.

'This is the man I dreamt of,' thought Kurmanjan,
But, despite this she was uneasy.
Her heart was pensive,
For Alymbek had a wife and child already.

244.

Nevertheless, Kurmanjan realised there was no escape,
Where could she go after leaving her husband?
Yet, when she ruminated on her plight,
Alymbek gazed at her with longing.

245.

'She is smart and well-bred,' Alymbek thought,
'If only she were my wife.'
So, examining traditions and conventions,
He attempted to fathom a future together.

246.

'She is as clever as Tolybay,' Alymbek thought,
'Her engaging words soften my heart.'
So deep in thought were they,
They didn't notice when they arrived in Japalak.

247.

Though Kurmanjan was shy before Datka,
She was animated and agitated equally.
She presented to him her embroidered handkerchief,
Stating, 'Do not forget, a lion safeguards this lady.'

248.

When Alymbek took hold
Of that sensational handkerchief,
He was enveloped in a passionate enchantment:
The pair were in awe of each other.

249.

Yet, their glances were tinged with melancholy,
As both wished they would never part anew.
Yet it was time to say adieu,
Which left a deep-rooted despair within each.

250.

'Goodbye,' said Alymbek, taking her hand,
And although shy, Kurmanjan returned the sentiment.
Faintly she said, 'See you later,'
And gave her hand to Alymbek.

KURMANJAN'S SONG

251.

'I gave you a handkerchief as a symbol of my love,
While you will use it to cleanse your face.
It has a distinctive illustration woven into it,
An image returning you to me when I miss you.

252.

'I gifted you with this handkerchief,
You will use it to wipe your hands.
It has magical properties,
Which you will discover when I long for you.'

253.

'The front of the kerchief,
Is adorned with green silk;
Reflecting an innocent love at first sight,
In a peculiar twist of fate.'

254.

'The back of the kerchief,
Is fashioned from pure red silk;
Since love dawned at first sight,
In a peculiar twist of fate.'

ALYMBEK'S SONG

255.

'Let me take your kerchief,
And keep it near my heart.
Let me place it in my breast pocket,
And when I miss you terribly,
I will use it and think of you.'

256.

'Let me take your handkerchief,
And keep it near my heart.
Let me put it in my left pocket,
And when I miss you terribly,
I will breathe in your scent.'

257.

'When I cast my eyes upon the kerchief,
It will cause my heart to ache.
When we miss each other,
I hope I will arrive for you in time.'

KURMANJAN RETURNS HOME

258.

Kurmanjan arrived in the village
Late in the evening and saw her parents.
It was unexpected for them, of course,
And, shocked, they asked, 'Why are you here?'

259.

Kurmanjan embraced her mother,
And, Aikan kissed her prodigal daughter.
The pair couldn't stop crying,
Since they had been apart for so long.

260.

Mamatbay was so astounded,
He could hardly speak.
Yet, restitution he must make to her husband for any dowry,
As a necessary but cruel penalty.

261.

'Let them take my cattle and whatever they wish.
I am joyous my daughter is safe and sound.'
Saying these words, he entered the house,
But, not to cry, weep or complain.

262.

He kissed and soothed poor Kurmanjan,
Holding her close and petting her head.
'While I'm still alive you won't cry anymore,
I promise, my dear,' he said.

263.

'It is enough that you are alive,
My dearest daughter,
Let Torokul come, I am ready.
If he comes with ill intent, I am prepared to resist him.'

264.

He pacified his wife and daughter,
Then Aikan laid out a bountiful spread.
'Let people talk, don't fret,
Rest my darling and worry not about them,' he said.

265.

It had been a long odyssey
And Kurmanjan was truly exhausted,
Hence, she slumbered and dreamt deeply,
As a babe in the cradle once more.

266.

In her dream, she saw a white yurt,
And Alymbek decked in a crisp white suit and hat.
People erected the yurt rapidly
Whereas rays spilt through the tunduk.

267.

With the national hat, the kalpak
Sitting high upon his head,
Alymbek strolled around the yurt
Which was thoroughly resplendent.

268.

Kurmanjan was rested after her repose.
She was ecstatic to see her parents well,
But the man that had crossed her path,
She knew she would never forget.

269.

Aikan enquired as to the reason,
Why Kurmanjan fled from the shackles of her marriage.
'It will be appalling when they come for you,
While did you take into account your family's honour?

270.

'They will say, your daughter has left her husband,
They will demand their dowry back.'
As Aikan finished her diatribe,
Kulseit and his men came-a-calling.

271.

Mamatbay went outside,
Greeting them with 'Salaam alaikum.'
'You must return the dowry,'
They said gruffly, spoiling for a fight.

272.

'Hand back all the silver, gold, and livestock,
And the bride must be made an example as well.
If you fail to meet our demands,
Kurmanjan will be restored to us.'

273.

Kurmanjan stepped outside, saying
'Welcome heroes to my house.
Despite all the silver and gold that was given,
And the Joosh tribe's entirety being ready for battle,
Kurmanjan will never return to Kulseit.'

274.

Kulseit became enraged and shouted at his soldiers,
'Take all their oxen if he doesn't relinquish her.'
Mamatbay then calmly unlocked his cattle shed,
Saying, 'Take them all,' with resolve.
'Take your silver, gold and precious stones.
Take your stallion and mare, take everything from me,
Because, I'll never give you my Kurmanjan!'

275.

Mamatbay gave all of his livestock to Kulseit,
Torokul took all of his wealth,
But he couldn't take Kurmanjan.
'Let my daughter be happy and have a long life,'
Mamatbay beseeched Great God.

276.

A year later, Mamatbay died.
Kurmanjan mourned for the longest time.
She was responsible for the remaining livestock,
And was in the pasture taking care of them,
That Alymbek continually flooded her thoughts.

277.

Alymbek also pined for her daily,
Whereas her words echoed throughout his mind,
Recounting a lady with a guardian lion.
He knew he would never forget her,
And stored thoughts of her in his heart.
Clearly, out of the blue, he would hold her kerchief,
And breathe in its sweet aroma.

278.

Alymbek was vexed with his wife;
He attempted to manage household relations,
Whilst feeling desolate inside
And unable to bear spending a night at home.

279.

He pretended to go fowling,
But instead looked for Kurmanjan on the jailoo.
He questioned locals about her location,
And engaged his staff in his quest.

280.

He scoured Kok Soo, Nura, Kusul Soo, Chong Alay
And the summer pasture at Ych- Chat,
Which bordered the neighbouring land of China.
He travelled through Nura, too.

281.

However, the scent of meadows and fresh mare's milk,
Yet again brought Kurmanjan to Alymbek's mind.
Thoughts of her had unsettled his life,
Whilst she languished for love of him too.

282.

The mild breeze of the Alay Range,
Assisted their passage down the Kok Soo River.
Alymbek was on his way to declare his love,
And ask Kurmanjan for her hand in marriage.

283.

When he arrived to ask for her hand,
He came upon a white funerary yurt.
A woman came out and he asked her
If this was Mamatbay's yurt.
She confirmed it was and went back inside; through the canvas
He heard Kurmanjan's mother's song of mourning.

AIKAN'S SONG OF MOURNING

284.

'The word death is never agreeable,
You will miss your beloved.
The word misery is not copacetic,
You have lost your dear one.'

285.

'O, my love, you wore a golden belt,
Your face was as charming as moonlight.
Now you don the golden belt no more,
For my darling, you've passed to the other world.'

286.

'O, my dear, you wore a silver belt,
Your face as radiant as sunlight.
Now you don the silver belt no more,
For my darling, you've passed to the other world.'

287.

'I awoke early, but there was no breeze,
I commemorate you, but there's no escape.
I awoke early, but there was no breeze,
I dream of you, but there's no escape.'

288.

'My beloved's foal grew to be a stallion,
He was the first rich man in the Mungush tribe.
His pasture was brimful with sheep,
He lived a joyful and wondrous life.'

289.

‘My beloved’s fields were teeming with wheat,
His hills were crowded with cattle.
He was not only cheerful, but empathetic,
Sharing his bounty with those less fortunate.’

290.

‘My beloved’s storehouse was replete with grain,
His meadows filled with livestock.
His tenacity and vigour
Was the stuff of legend.’

291.

‘My darling was constantly on his racehorse, Akbay,
His clothes were gilded with silver.
Now, Akbay has no rider,
My dearest Mamat is no more.’

292.

‘Let me mourn no more,
Let my love be in paradise.
Let me mourn no more,
Let my love be in paradise.’

293.

Alymbek prayed for the soul of the departed,
And that his widow be calmed and consoled.
Kurmanjan watched silently on,
But shortly could not contain her emotions.
Everything she had bottled inside
Uncontrollably bursting forth.

294.

Aikan observed Alymbek,
And intuited he had not come by chance.
So, perceiving the meaningful look in his eyes
And the charged atmosphere in the air,
She recalled Kurmanjan's words.

295.

It had been a struggle to escape Kulseit,
Their marriage a bane to endure.
The river had been wild and tumultuous,
But she'd overcome all to cross it.

296.

The Red Lion had watched over her,
Carrying her out of the river's clutches;
Five lions had granted safe passage,
By providence, she had survived.

297.

Afterwards, she had met a traveller,
And clearly, it had been Alymbek Datka,
This leonine fellow she had encountered
Seemed like her guardian spirit.

298.

She'd given him her handkerchief,
So, he would not forget her.
He'd escorted her to the outskirts of Japalak.
Thus, Aikan withdrew to give them space.

299.

Alymbek expressed his prayers and condolences,
Whilst they sipped on kumis.
'I must give you time to grieve,' he said,
'I will ask for your hand in a year and a day.'

300.

Kurmanjan lamented the loss of her father,
And with tears of bereavement
Streaming down her face
She could barely answer Alymbek's words.

301.

It was hard to wait a year and a day,
They yearned for each other desperately.
Their days passed into emptiness:
Their hearts filled with unsated desires.

302.

It was difficult for them to meet,
The law was rigid about their interactions.
It was almost impossible to be alone together,
There was no way for him to get a divorce.

303.

'If fate allowed us to convene,' Alymbek thought,
'We would relish our time together.
Thence, I could declare my love,
And ask for her hand in marriage.'

304.

'Let me visit Japalak as soon as possible,
Let me be reunited with the leonine lady.
Let me procure the blessing of my in-laws, thought Alymbek,
Drafting a letter for this express purpose.'

305.

His parents blessed him cordially.
They wished him happiness and a fruitful journey.
'Let this wife be keen and wise,' they said,
'Let our son be content and prosperous with her.'

306.

With their benediction, he started on his way,
To his beloved Kurmanjan.
'Is she aware of my feelings?' he wondered,
'Will she agree to be my bride?'

307.

He arrived in Japalak with his men,
To ask her hand in marriage.
If God would permit them to take their vows,
He would speak his words of devotion.

308.

He arrived in Japalak with his men,
To ask for the hand of his future spouse.
After they had greeted him with high tea,
There was an opportunity to talk.

ALYMBEK DATKA'S WORDS

309.

'Let me admire the way you walk,
Let me sip kumis with you and talk.
I watch your movements, so graceful.
Let me drink from your elegant hands.'

310.

'Let me enjoy your gait in the street,
Let me sip kumis with you and talk.
Let me wait upon you and look forward to
Drinking bozo from your hands.'

311.

'On the roof of your house,
Let me build a nest,
Let me afford you no peace;
Let me appear in your dreams.'

312.

'On the roof of your house,
Let me nest like a lark,
Let us suit each other, regardless,
Let us soon be wed.'

313.

'On the gambrel of your palace,
Let me land like an eagle,
With you as a white swan entwined with me;
Let us soon be wed.'

314.

'Let us have a castle in Alay.
Before your Mother,
I will ask for your hand;
And make our engagement official.'

KURMANJAN'S WORDS

315.

'If you return to me every day,
I'll have your kumis ready.
Although I've been wed previously,
I'm ready for a new engagement.'

316.

'If you alight upon my roof,
I'll allow you into my dreams.
May you be my husband,
As prophesied in my vision.'

317.

'If you choose to land on my white palace,
Let me fill you with wonder.
May you be my husband,
As prophesied in my vision.'

318.

'I can't help but say it again,
Divorce is taboo amongst our people;
But, I have suffered through that separation
And there is no other way.'

319.

'When I first saw a gallant knight such as you,
My heart was set aflutter.
Why couldn't we have met before
I was married to Kulseit?'

320.

'As a married woman,
It is a grave sin to separate.
Even a Khan of Kokand can't marry me,
According to Sharia law.'

321.

'If you find a way to divorce,
Then I will be glad to wed you.
Blameless if your wife would withdraw,
Then we can be married.'

322.

'If you dissolve your marriage,
Then I will be glad to wed you.
We may be breaking with tradition,
But then you can ask for my hand in matrimony.'

ALYMBEK DATKA'S REPLY

323.

'Both of us have previously been married,
In this our fate and fortune show symmetry.
But, if our hearts won't accept each other,
There is nothing to be done.'

324.

"There is no precedent of divorce in our culture,
Even when a match is unsuited.
We have no other option, however,
We cannot live with regret.'

325.

'I would not go through these trials to marry you,
If I didn't truly love and respect you.
You are not to be blamed
For leaving your loveless husband.'

326.

'Even though you were married, you are wise,
So, let me relate to you as a single girl.
Let me make a feast that lasts for thirty days,
Let me make a wedding celebration that lasts for forty days.'

327.

'I will invite Torokul's son,
I will plead your case.
Then, let judges analyse and decide
On Kulseit's moral and physical aptitude!
Thereafter, you will be divorced legitimately,
And receive your freedom.'

328.

Alymbek made an offering Kulseit,
To choose any woman he wanted.
Alymbek would pay her dowry for him,
If Kulseit should choose to marry again.

329.

'If you separate from Kurmanjan,' he said,
'Then you shall also be free.
There are many girls well-suited
For you to make a fortuitous match.'

330.

Alymbek addressed Kulseit thus,
And Kulseit agreed.
'If Datka will pay the dowry,' he said,
'I will leave forthwith for Katty-Bagyt Kashkarga,
And pursue for myself a new bride.'

331.

Kurmanjan was overjoyed by the news
Knowing she was free from Kulseit.
Now she could do as she pleased,
She was satisfied with Datka.

332.

'I have fulfilled my promise,'
Spoke Alymbek to Kurmanjan,
'Now I await your answer.'

333.

'Thank you, my dear Datka,' she replied,
'I will also keep my promise to you,
But, I have one condition:
Forty yurts are to be erected on the banks of the Ak-Buura;
Let forty girls accompany me,
Let everyone come to our feast.
And let it last for forty days.'

334.

'I can meet your demands,' said Alymbek,
'My parents will come to your family.
They will bring nine different types of cattle,
They will bring silver and gold,
They will pay the dowry of my beautiful bride.'

335.

They discussed the wedding,
And Kurmanjan explained
That her Uncle Ismadiyar,
Would make all of the arrangements.

336.

Alymbek's parents came to Japalak,
And went to Ismadiyar's house with the bride-to-be.
They blessed the couple's union,
And began preparations for the ceremony.

THE BEGINNING OF THE FEAST

337.

All were welcome to the nuptials.
Let people enjoy their celebrations.
The feast will last for forty days
And it was organised by Alymbek and Ismadiyar.

338.

All are welcome to the celebration,
For those who'll come from Andijan,
A bear skin rug has been prepared
On which they will be seated.

339.

The feast will commence, all are welcome;
Let the people come and savour it.
Let them be exultant
As they give their blessings to the couple.

340.

All are welcome to the wedding;
Kurmanjan is a splendid bride,
Alymbek a model of sophistication,
The hosts in high spirits both.

341.

You are welcome, dear in-laws,
May God provide for you.
This bride and groom are well-suited,
Truly, a match made in heaven.

342.

Let our honoured guests take their places,
So, the wedding feast can begin.
First, there is the ritual of Ala kachuu:
The groom must seek out his intended.

343.

Let us look for the bride,
Let Alymbek's friends assist in the search,
But if the groom queries her relatives,
They will never reveal her location.

344.

The groom's friend accompanies every search songfully.
A talented vocalist for the gala,
He can play the fretless komuz with skill,
And sing with the voice of a seraph.

THE KOMUZ PLAYER'S SONG

345.

'It is a tradition amongst our people,
For the bride will hide before the feast.
Where could they have sequestered her?
Where can my dear friend find her?'

346.

'The guests have arrived with
Countless gifts: a stash of
Golden coins are brimming.
Please, show us where the bride is, dear girl.'

347.

‘There are grand offerings for the house;
And for the girl who helped her hide
Yet, there is a silver coin if you will
Reveal the bride’s hiding place, dear girl.’

348.

‘It’s our tradition to hide the bride,’
The girl responded, ‘we’ve hidden her well.
You, who are looking for the bride,
Where she is we will never tell.’

349.

‘What gift do you require to surrender her?
What do you require, dear girl?
For we are eager to see the bride,
Please, take us to her immediately!’

350.

‘What gift do you require to surrender her?
What do you require, dear girl?
For we are eager to see the bride,
Let’s go to her together.’

351.

‘In order to behold the bride,’ she replied,
‘We do not wish for your silver,
But, we would like to see
What the groom will offer her.’

352.

‘In order to behold the bride,
We do not wish for your gold,
But, we are dying to witness the prowess
Of all the fellows present here.’

353.

So, the girls brought out Kurmanjan
Decked in a white wedding cap.
The ceremony of seeing the bride
Was ready to begin.

354.

‘They say you have black eyebrows,’
The komuz player sang.
‘Let me gift you cosmetics,
To beautify your brows.’

355.

'They say that your eyes are black,
Let me see your eyes.
Let me gift you cosmetics,
So that your eyes may sparkle.'

356.

'They say you have long hair,
Let me see your hair,
Let me gift you a bejewelled pin,
For your captivating hair.'

357.

'They say your face is angelic,
Let me see your face.
Let me gift you powder and lipstick,
To fashion your charming face.'

KURMANJAN'S SISTER-IN-LAW'S SONG

358.

'Your beautifully painted eyebrows,
Will lose their lustre if you wipe them;
But, your injured soul will be cured,
If you love someone truly.'

359.

'Your beautifully painted eyelashes,
Will lose their lustre if you wipe them;
But if you have found true love,
You will live without regrets.'

360.

'Kurmanjan, I ask of you
To reveal your raven hair,
Then place in it this decorous hairpin
And enjoy an entwined life together.'

361.

'Kurmanjan has a natural radiance,
So, gaze upon her and bask in it, my brother.
Your beloved, Kurmanjan
Will be your devoted wife.'

THE WEDDING FEAST

362.

Thus, the people celebrated;
Alymbek had fulfilled his obligations
And paid a hefty dowry.
The guests played different national sports,
Such as catch the girl and wrestling
For the next forty days.

363.

Kyz kuu is a provocative pastime,
In which a man captures a girl on a horse.
If a girl seizes a boy, though,
She will lash him with a whip.

364.

During the wedding party
On the banks of the Ak-Buura,
One girl lost at Kyz kuu,
But, the contest inspired this feast
As the couple found they were suited
And shortly, there would be another wedding.

365.

At night, young people played Ak Cholmok,
Searching for a thrown
White stick and calling
Out each other's names.

366.

This was another time-honoured diversion,
In which new acquaintances are made.
Sometimes a good match is found
And will result in marriage.

367.

Divided into two teams, the players
Will shout, 'Ak Cholmok' in turn,
And whichever team finds the white stick
Is considered to be the winner.

368.

There is a similar game
Called Jooluk Salmai
In which young people search for a handkerchief
Yet, oftentimes find their true love instead.

369.

In order that they live full lives,
There are so many national games
That develop the abilities of the young
And are valued by the people.

370.

As the children played,
Bards sang a song praising the happy couple.
When girls finished their verses,
It was the boy's turn to answer.

371.

There is another game called Shakek Salmai,
Where one sings whilst placing rings on others fingers.
Still, when the vocalist sings 'a golden ring,'
The person who received the last ring must sing.
This game develops musical abilities
And helps find the best singers in the community.

372.

Sarmerden is a contest of singers
Held between all the young boys and girls.
The boys sing of the girl's beauty and abilities,
While eaxing eloquently on how
They will respect their future spouse
And raise children in a house filled with love
Suchwise upholds traditions in our Kyrgyz nation.

373.

In a Sarmerden contest,
Boys and girls sit facing each other,
The boys reciting tongue-twisters
Which speak of their respect and generosity.

374.

This aspect of Sarmerden,
Is a test of memory
Set to discover the
Most intelligent in the land.

375.

There is a special part of the game called 'exaggeration,'
Which trains young people in articulation,
Whereas, the audience are set to judge whether
The speaker's words are true or false.

376.

Everyone enjoyed the wedding
On the banks of the Ak-Buura.
Indeed, people came from all over the land
To partake in this feast.
Their national games were played
While building treasured memories forever.
If anyone researches further,
They will find more and more jewels.

SEEING OFF THE BRIDE

377.

She wears golden rings,
She grew up in a shady place.
She wears silver rings,
She grew up in the shadows.

378.

Please give her golden rings,
To glisten in shady places.
Please give her silver rings,
To guard her through the shadows.

379.

She is as clever as…
Let her be Datka's good wife;
And her beloved Alymbek,
She will charm as the moon.

380.

She is as wise as…
Let her be Datka's good wife;
And before adoring Alymbek,
Let her sparkle like the sun.

381.

Let her radiant rays cover him;
Taking care of his lady like the moon.
Let her radiant rays cover him;
Taking care of his lady like the sun.

382.

There is a shining path for you;
May you be the mother of a daughter.
There is an unbroken path for you;
May you be the mother of a son.

383.

Let her not speak roughly,
So, that she would offend her mother-in-law;
Let her not speak thoughtlessly,
So, that she would upset her father-in-law.

384.

Be a virtuous woman in your new family,
Let your husband be proud of you.
Be a shining example to your new family,
Let your in-laws be gladdened.

385.

When you walk through your new palace,
May your gait be jaunty.
Lady of the guardian lion,
May your days be full.

386.

When the couple rode off side by side,
She in a white parchcha dress and cap,
Her accessories of gold and silver
Were dazzling in the sun.

387.

'The lovers are well-suited,'
Young people whispered to each other;
'Let God always protect them
From the evil eye.'

388.

Her long hair is decorous,
Her white dress billows in the wind;
Her cap greets the snowy mountains
As does Alymbek's white kalpak.

389.

Alay is still far off,
Yet, they arrived at a hot spring,
Whereby was erected a white yurt
Which was truly resplendent.

390.

Kurmanjan washed her face and rested,
Whilst Alymbek attended
To her needs,
A sign of his respect.

391.

The sky was cobalt blue, the moon illuminating
Alymbek's entourage
As they decamped
For the night.

392.

Such was Alymbek's retinue
That they pitched another forty yurts.
The valley then filled with laughter and games
As the bards strummed on their komuz instruments.

A SPECIAL SONG BEFORE THE WEDDING PARTY

393.

'From the sacred city of Osh,
There came a bride, jar-jar-ai.
She made a graceful bow
To the people of Alay, jar-jar-ai.'

394.

'From sacred Sulayman Mountain,
There came a bride, jar-jar-ai.
She made a courteous bow
To her father-in-law, jar-jar-ai.'

395.

‘From hallowed Kerme-Too,
There came a bride, jar-jar-ai.
She made a polite greeting
To her mother in law, jar-jar-ai.’

396.

‘From the banks of the Ak-Buura,
There came a bride, jar-jar-ai.
She treated the people of Alay
With great respect, jar-jar-ai.’

397.

‘There is a belt as handsome as
Good Alymbek, jar-jar-ai.
There is a lady who matches him,
A striking woman, jar-jar-ai.’

398.

‘There is a belt for Datka
That becomes him, jar-jar-ai.
There is a spouse for Datka
Who completes him, jar-jar-ai.’

399.

'She is Ak-Burra's beauty,
Married and blissful, jar-jar-ai.
He is the hero of the people of Alay,
Who has found his beloved, jar-jar-ai.'

400.

'They are a perfect couple,
All people admire them, jar-jar-ai.
Let God protect them
From the evil eye.'

401.

'Before the entrance of a White Palace,
Let them enjoy their lives, jar-jar-ai.
Let their marriage be harmonious;
Burn juniper for their success.'

402.

'Let juniper cleanse any bad omens,
Let her be one with the family, jar-jar-ai.
Let the scent of juniper
Eradicate grave tidings.'

403.

'Let the new bride place a white kerchief
On her head, jar-jar-ai.
Let her taste the melted butter
And be received into the household.'

THE NEWLYWEDS ARRIVE IN ALAY

404.

All the people of Alay
Accompanied the newlyweds to the palace,
Saying 'now he has found his true match,
Let their marriage be consummated.'

405.

'This woman outstrips his first bride,
She is worthy of our attention.
It was their destiny to meet,
Let their marriage be consummated.'

406.

'She was destined to be the daughter-in-law
Of the Alay people.
She respects her in-laws according to tradition
Serving young and old alike.'

407.

'She is a wise lady; people can believe in her
And trust her advice.
She is a special lady,
She truly is outstanding.'

408.

Kurmanjan was generous and kind,
Spreading her God-given light.
People began to tell stories about
Her compassion and benevolence.

409.

Kurmanjan's mind worked differently from others,
Since she had the gift of foresight.
Sometimes she shocked her husband
With her unrivalled prescience.

410.

Their days were sweet and full;
They were busy, but satisfied.
When they faced a problem,
They would reach a decision together.

411.

Time passed, but Kurmanjan
Did not conceive, which saddened her.
She prayed to God that she might
Bear a child for Alymbek.

412.

Alymbek's sister, Uuljan visited Alay,
Her brother ordering a golden cradle made
For her baby which Kurmanjan would take care of.
Enjoying the scent of the baby,
Kurmanjan grew impatient to have a child of her own.

413.

Kurmanjan thought only
About being with child.
When the couple chanced upon an orphan,
They adopted him and named him Karabek.

414.

Raised in a loving home, that baby was the happiest,
Whilst Kurmanjan thought she would surely become pregnant.
It is a belief throughout the land
That if you adopt a child, another will appear.

415.

Nobody was to tell Karabek that he was adopted;
Alymbek raised him as if he were his own blood.
Certainly, if somebody dared to utter this secret
They would be punished most harshly.

416.

Their abiding wish soon came to pass,
And Kurmanjan became pregnant.
She gave birth to a boy
Who they named Abdyldabek.

417.

First, they celebrated the Cradle Feast.
Then the Cutting of the Knot.
When Abdyldabek was five: following tradition
They had him circumcised.

418.

Kurmanjan bore seven children, five sons and two daughters.
Abdyldabek, Kamchybek, Mamatbek
Asanbek and Omorbek the boys were named.
Their daughters, Aiymbubu and Satinbubu
Were like their Mother, the finest of ladies.

419.

Datka already had two sons with his first wife
Whom he raised wonderfully.
They had good relations
With their new brothers and sisters.

420.

It was the time of the Kokand Khans
In the mid- nineteenth century.
Alymbek was in the post of biy,
Keeping peace and unity among the people
And safeguarding the nation from invaders.

421.

Both of them thought long and hard
About the future of the Kyrgyz nation,
Though due to palace intrigues
Alymbek was often away.

422.

Alymbek visited Alay when he could
And saw that Kurmanjan was the right lady,
That she guided the people honestly
With both charm and wisdom.

423.

Kurmanjan was eager
To see more of her husband,
But, never complained when he had to depart:
Seeing him off with kind words.

424.

When he arrived from Kokand tired and sad,
She met him with compassion.
Their house was always immaculate
And she a willing listener.

425.

'Whilst you were in Kokand, my dear'
She told him patiently,
'I tried to find solutions
To the problems which arose.'

426.

'I fulfilled my duties guided by thoughts
Of what would be your actions and words.
I prayed for God to keep you safe,
My beloved, my friend and truest advisor.'

427.

‘There may be ups and downs in the fortunes of the nation:
People may come to ask for my assistance.
There may be trials and tribulations
Over which I try to decide with honesty and sincerity.’

428.

‘Don’t trouble yourself, you must be tired;
Don’t trouble yourself, all is well.
I will explain everything to you
After you have rested a little.’

429.

‘Well done, my darling, I am
Satisfied,’ said Alymbek,
‘I can see you’ve performed your tasks diligently
Whilst I’ve been away.’

430.

‘You are welcome, my dear, my knight,’ she replied,
‘I am honoured to serve your nation.
As long as you believe in me,
I’ll strive with every fibre of my body and soul
To make the people feel as if you were here.’

431.

It warmed his heart to hear her words
As he looked into her shining eyes.
He always had such a wonderful time
With Kurmanjan in Alay.

432.

All the people blessed Alymbek Datka,
His authority and esteem rising ever higher;
Kurmanjan always felt heavenly
As a helper to her Datka.

ALL ABOUT ALYMBEK DATKA

433.

'Who knows what the baby in the cradle will become,'
Is a proverb of the nation.
Albeit, Asanbiy's son, Alymbek who
Continued with his father's historic vocation.

434.

Baibocho from Bokoy, Tilekke from
Baibocho, Ajybek from Tilekke,
All received the blessings of the people.
Independently and freely,

Alymbek took care of the nation
As his forefathers had done.

435.

From the tribe of Adigene,
One of forty tribes of the Kyrgyz nation,
For generations Alymbek's
Forebears had been leaders.

436.

Tilekke's eight grandsons were
Intelligent, kind and judicious.
They fought for the freedom
Not only of Osh, but the whole of Ferghana.

437.

Ajybek was the leader of an independent nation
Who commanded much respect.
It was a period of senseless murders
When the Khan's power was cruel,
And Alymbek's honest ancestry
Saved countless lives.

438.

Ajybek fought against enemies and invaders,
Against those who wanted to take their land.
Independent from both Qing and Kokand,
He devoted his life to his nation.

439.

Ajybek enlisted twenty thousand warriors
For the fight against Irdana-biy.
Many died on that battlefield,
Whilst others languished in prisons.

440.

They couldn't keep Ajybek in shackles, though:
If Qing was to ally with him there would be a new war.
By special decree, he was released.
However, Irdana-biy liked to show his sword,
Although didn't always know how to wield it.

441.

Ajybek soon gathered all the leaders of the tribes:
To Adigene, Mongol, Karabagysh and Sayaks alike
He said, 'We must unite, we are Kyrgyz brothers
Who must fight against the enemies of our freedom and honour.'

442.

Wanting to take lands in Central Asia,
The Chinese army marched forth
And Ajybek made a pact
With Irdana-biy of Kokand.

443.

It was the middle of the nineteenth century,
The Dzungar Khans and Qing soldiers
Spilt into Central Asia,
But Ajybek's warriors united to rebuff them.

444.

Despite his great endeavours,
Ajybek was injured.
A Dzungar warrior shot him
And Ajybek died a hero.

445.

The Kyrgyz nation saw its son depart for the next world.
The blue flag of the region flew at half-mast.
As the symbol of mourning, while women still wear blue
Dresses as a tradition that dates from that time.

446.

People said prayers from the Kuran
For their fallen hero;
But his grandson, Alymbek
Was proud of his heritage.

447.

When we speak of Alymbek,
History recalls his name;
He became the Vice-Khan of Kokand
Standing fearlessly against marauders.

448.

It was in his blood to defend the motherland,
As it was with every person an unwritten law;
Indeed, the Kyrgyz nation was united
Because of Alymbek's diplomacy and wisdom.

449.

The headmen of the forty tribes
Were as one, like the rafters of a yurt.
Proudly hanging their flags ever higher,
They didn't think of their own wealth and power,
But were unified under leonine Alymbek.

450.

Convening a meeting in Kokand,
They defined the borders of every region:
Alay, Osh, the province of Andijan,
Tashkent and Namangan. From the prairie hills to the plains,
Castles and great defensive walls were constructed.

451.

Tax officers sent by the Khan of Kokand
Placed a great burden upon the people, however.
Taking by force peoples horses,
Cattle and provisions.

452.

The whole population of the Ferghana Valley
Were prepared for civil disobedience.
Alymbek rallied to their side, saying
'Kyrgyz people will never be slaves.'
They fought for their freedom from 1827,
Amid fields drenched in blood for four long years.

453.

The Kokand Khan was afraid that
The Kyrgyz people would win their independence.
He wanted to retain his unrivalled importance
For caravans on the Silk Road.

454.

Yet, the Kyrgyz tribes were strong,
And Kyrgyz people held important positions
Throughout the Khanate,
With Alymbek as a shining example.

455.

It was a time of patriarchy,
When women were subject to strenuous requirements
And not allowed to leave their houses
Without a man's permission.

456.

It was Alymbek who changed this,
Saying a woman's place should be higher than tradition.
He gave his wife a palace to govern
While leading the people of Alay.

457.

Presenting Kurmanjan with his silver whip,
He advised her that to be a good ruler
People sometimes act like children,
And she would need to show them her whip.

458.

'You have to rule in my stead,' he told her,
'Yes, my dear King,' she agreed.
'And I won't trouble you without reason,
But should I send you the whip
It's a sign that there's great danger.'

459.

The Kokand's Khan imposed taxes upon
The people of Alay and the Pamir.
Aggressive in seeking their fortune,
Tax collectors arrived at the Palace of Adigene.

460.

Asanbiy's children were against the taxes.
They didn't accept the edict of the Khan.
Instead, refusing to allow his men passage.
So, the Kokand soldiers returned home empty-handed.

461.

Madali-Khan knew that he couldn't win,
And the only way was to make good relations;
To involve the Kyrgyz blue bloods.
Hence, he invited them to dine, and awarded
Them titles like Datka and Pansat.

462.

For his governance within his nation,
Alymbek was awarded the title, Datka.
On a scroll marked with a special stamp
That was handed to him by the Khan.

463.

Still, Madali-Khan was not satisfied.
He wanted to extend his power in the north,
Yet, the tribes united against him,
To stop him from fulfilling his dream.

464.

War with Bukhara brought misfortune to Madali,
Who saw his army routed.
Whereas Istaravshan and Khojend were lost
To the Emir Nasrullah.

465.

Madali Khan and his relatives,
His sons, mother, brothers
And his most famous bard
Were captured by the enemy.

466.

Nasrullah was known for his cruelty
And the prisoners were executed.
The Emir then announced by decree,
Ibrahim-Dadhoh of Bukhara would be the Khan of Kokand.

467.

As soon as Ibrahim-Dadhoh came into power
He ordered an increase in taxes,
His officers tormented the people,
Plundering these lands.

468.

A plan was hatched in secret.
Representatives coming from far and wide;
Their armies would unite
And with God's help force the Emir's man out.

469.

So, Kyrgyz and Kipchaks united
And went together to sacred Safed-Bulan,
Where according to the tradition of their ancestors,
They placed Shir Ali on a white felt,
Saying 'let God support us, let him be the new Khan.'

470.

The nomadic Kyrgyz people,
Accepting Shir Ali as their noble ancestor
Brought him from Talas to Kokand
And nominated him as Khan in his fiftieth year.

471.

Shir Ali was placed upon the throne,
But, his boots were left nearby
So, he would remember that
He'd once been a humble breeder of cattle.

472.

Shir Ali came to Kokand in a hurry,
Hot on the heels of Ibrahim-Dadhoh.
Nevertheless, the land was in flux,
With Madali-Khan's remaining entourage
Behaving like snakes in the water.

473.

Madali-Khan's men were captured and punished
By the new Khan from Talas.
Born in such a holy place
And a clear ancestor of our hero, Manas.

474.

Shir Ali Khan supported the Kyrgyz nation,
And took the throne for this reason.
In deciding the policies of Kokand,
Kyrgyz people took a leading role.

475.

Involving all the blue blood and biys,
The Khan surrounded himself with wise advisors.
Alymbek was one these people
Supporting Shir Ali as the Khan of the Kyrgyz.

476.

Unable to manage the workload of a Khan,
Shir Ali appointed Musulmankul as his vizier.
Yet, Musulmankul became a despot beyond his vocation,
Raising taxes and ignoring the people.

477.

Musulmankul took each power in his hands,
Thereby, dismissing Alymbek from office:
Hanging people turned into a simple job,
Whereas, the killing of innocents customary.

478.

People could barely believe what was happening
And were once again
On the verge of revolt,
Ready to strike against the Khan.

479.

Kurmanjan perceived everything in time.
Musulmankul was blameworthy for these machinations.
'We have to keep Shir Ali as Khan
And restore his reputation with the people,' she wrote
Sending a rider with a message for Alymbek.

480.

After listening to her missive, Alymbek
Gathered people from Alay, Osh and Pamir
For a foray against Musulmankul.
He himself would lead the revolution.

MUSULMANKUL'S LETTER TO THE SECRET SERVICE AND THE TRIBES

481.

'If you find Alymbek, kill him immediately,
If you can't do it, I will do it myself.
Tie his hands and don't give a damn for him;
I will chop off his head myself.'

482.

'To the head of the tribe, Seitbek Datka.
Don't be hasty and support Alymbek;

To the head of the Kesek tribe,
Don't be Alymbek's slaves or servants.'

MUSULMANKUL'S LETTER TO ALYMBEK

483.

'Dear Alymbek, you are not a hero,
With only one wing an eagle is not airborne
And we were two wings of this government,'
He wrote before leaving to pursue Alymbek
With murder in his heart.

EVENTS UNFOLD

484.

The people made a plan during these times:
They would kill Musulmankul
Who treated them contemptuously
And be free from the aggression of Kokand.

485.

Though they had few weapons,
They fought gallantly
And killed many of the Khan's soldiers.
Yet, it was no use and they were defeated.

Thence, the streets of Osh were awash with blood,
While ten thousand were taken prisoner.

486.

Arriving in Kokand, Musulmankul had plans for murder,
But, loyal Jarkynaim knew and sent a rider to Kurmanjan.
'Musulmankul is preparing to kill Alymbek,' he wrote.
'Let his plans be ruined,
It is only you who can save him from death,
May God help you in this.'

487.

Upon receiving the news, Kurmanjan concocted a scheme
On how to save her husband from this fate.
She sent the silver whip to Alymbek,
As a secret sign he should come post-haste.

488.

'Please take it to him instantly,'
She beseeched the messenger.
'I do not wish to see my people in tears;
Let Alymbek be safe.'

489.

On the battlefield, Alymbek
Was greatly concerned upon receiving the silver whip.

He knew he should leave immediately,
Even though it was the dead of night.

490.

Across a field wet with blood,
He saw Musulmankul therein.
Alymbek was ready to fight,
But, Kurmanjan's rider insisted they leave.

491.

'Who knows the state of affairs in Alay,' he thought,
'Are there enemies in my palace?
What about Kurmanjan and our children;
Have aggressors occupied my land? '

492.

And so he arrived in Alay,
And taking Kurmanjan's hand in his,
Asked of his beautiful wife
Why she had sent the silver whip.

493.

'Yes, I summoned you, my love,
There was a pressing reason for your return:
I would like to save your life from your enemy,
That's why I sent the silver whip.'

494.

'Does death stalk me, my love?' he asked,
Before Kurmanjan explained everything.
Alymbek prepared his warriors,
Giving thanks that Jarkynaim had delivered the message in time.

495.

Satisfied with her wisdom and delicacy,
The secret service had worked well for him.
He hugged his wife and looked upon her lovingly
Whilst Musulmankul grew frantic.

496.

The revolution in Osh was a calamity,
With massive losses incurred on both sides.
Yet, Musulmankul wanted to take the advantage,
By convening a meeting to select a new Khan,
At which he nominated Murad Beg.

497.

Undoubtedly, Musulmankul had invited each head,
Telling them to keep the meeting secret.
Murad Beg would be the Khan of Kokand
And pay Shir Ali a fatal visit.

498.

Together with his warriors,
Retinue and bodyguards,
Murad Beg came to Kokand
To be crowned as Khan.

499.

To take Shir Ali from his throne,
Musulmankul waited for the dread moment
And kept his silence silent about
Who had dealt the lethal blow.

500.

Murad Beg sat in the throne for only eleven days;
It was his fate, given by God,
Yet, if his dream was to be Khan
It had been fulfilled.

501.

Upon the demise of Murad Beg,
Shir Ali's son, Khudayar was placed on the white felt
And, thereafter, ascended the throne
At the tender age of sixteen.

502.

Musulmankul dominated the child Khan;
His rule over the country complete,
He bestowed titles upon himself
And married his daughter to Khudayar.

503.

Musulmankul ruthlessly purged the elites,
Slaughtering rivals without remorse.
Khudayar wished to be close to the Kyrgyz people,
But was effectively a prisoner of his father-in-law.

504.

Khudayar Khan took advice from his mother
Jatkunaim; a lady most wise,
Who took her counsel from the people,
Although Musulmankul retained the reins of power.

505.

Khudayar Khan had loved hunting since childhood,
Spending his time in the open air.
He travelled to Alay to recuperate,
Drinking mare's milk and resting.

506.

They came to Alay in the summer,
Setting up camp for ninety days.
Kurmanjan and Jatkunaim grew close,
And consulted each other on affairs of state.

507.

Musulmankul grew ever greedier,
By imposing a birth tax on newborns.
The people became disaffected
And once again ready to revolt.

508.

Musulmankul wanted to keep Khudayar isolated,
In a position with no power over Khanate finances;
Then, Musulmankul alone would be master of the treasury,
While Khudayar the Khan in name only.

509.

As he matured into an adult,
Khudayar became sick of his father-in-law;
Contrarily, he knew who he was and what he stood for,
And began to feel a sense of patriotism.

510.

Khudayar Khan rose up against his father-in-law.
For three months they fought, twenty thousand died.
Yet, Musulmankul and his inner circle were imprisoned
Whereas, Kipchak elites were eliminated before their eyes.

511.

Musulmankul was killed.
The palace was purged of Kipchaks.
Uzbeks and Tajiks took the highest positions,
As Russia and England turned their eyes to Central Asia.

512.

The Russian Empire advanced
With the goal of controlling the region.
As Russian incursions continued,
The power of Kokand was divided.

513.

Mallya Beg would unseat his stepbrother, Khudayar,
But had no army to speak of.
So, seeking assistance from Alymbek,
They collected a thousand warriors.

514.

They set out for Andijan together,
To take the Kokand Khanate:
Brother fought against brother,
And the vanquished Khudayar fled to Bukhara.

515.

Alymbek was appointed vizier,
And did his utmost for the Kyrgyz people,
Yet, once Mallya Beg took the throne
His behaviour was no different from his predecessors.

516.

The power of Kokand was divided,
Whilst Russia looked on with envious eyes;
They wanted to have cheap meats, fruits and leather,
As well as to take natural resources.

517.

A so-called Scientific Expedition from Russia arrived
And the Kyrgyz treated them hospitably:
Feasting them on the apples and apricots from Ferghana
And pure cool water from mountain springs.

518.

The Russians decided to move quickly,
Besieging the castles of Kokand;
Hence, Mallya Beg ordered Alymbek not to cede land
To which he agreed, though the enemy was strong.

519.

All the white beards discussed strategies:
The old ladies prayed to God
To bless their fine young men
Who would battle for their freedom.

520.

'We must be united against,' said Kurmanjan,
'As a hero of our nation.
Oh, my dear Alymbek, we pray for you;
Your sons and daughters wish for your safe return.'

521.

Alymbek departed with his soldiers.
The prayers of the people ringing in their ears.
But, presently, they met with Kanat Shah of Tashkent,
Who did not agree to join their forces.

522.

Alymbek espied the Russian Army:
Thousands of soldiers who were ready to fight.
They had modern weapons and uniforms,
They had huge reserves of gunpowder.

523.

Kanat Shah didn't consider his duties
As a leader of the nation.
He refused to heed Alymbek's advice
And so his men died in vain.

524.

Alymbek didn't engage the enemy,
For it was a battle he could not win.
He didn't give his men's lives in vain
And make their mothers or widows weep.

525.

He saved the life of ten thousand men
By withdrawing them from the field.
Why should the brave Kyrgyz die
For the sake of the Kokand Khan?

526.

The Kokand Khan's took taxes from villagers and
Caravans passing through Osh-Alay;
Why should the brave Kyrgyz die
For the throne of the Kokand Khanate?

527.

Khan Mallya Beg's historian
Wrote harsh words about Alymbek
And Kanat Shah travelled to Kokand
Asking that Alymbek be punished.

528.

But, did Mallya Beg dare punish him?
He was so respected in Alay.
Time passed, but the Khan harboured a grudge,
Forgetting it was Alymbek who'd supported his ascension.

529.

Mallya Beg plotted against Alymbek,
Yet, Kurmanjan's prescience thwarted him.
While he lived among the Kyrgyz people,
The blue bloods of the Sarbagysh tribe
Were his staunchest supporters.

530.

The Russians occupied Kokand
And Mallya Beg sent ambassadors
To ask Alymbek for assistance,
But, Alymbek didn't trust them or listen to their overtures.

531.

The Governor-General of Western Siberia,
Dugamel, had heard tales of Alymbek,
And thought that Alymbek might ask for help
To become a leader of the Kyrgyz People.

532.

If we relate well to Alymbek, he reasoned,
Caravans will pass without problems.
The Kashgar Highway will be perpetually open,
If we offer Alymbek our support.

533.

The Minister of Foreign Affairs of the Russian Empire
Was Gorchakov at that time! He relayed orders
To Dugamel from Emperor Alexander the Second
To offer the said assistance.

534.

Alymbek thought it was high time to establish the Kyrgyz State,
And ruminated often upon this idea.
'It's my personal duty to the motherland,' he thought,
'That we should not be the slaves of others.'

535.

Alymbek didn't collect gold and silver for himself,
He didn't differentiate between rich and poor.
He only wished to rule honestly
And establish independence.

536.

He had worked hard as vizier
To create equality
Yet, in doing so, had made
Enemies amongst the wealthy.

537.

The Kyrgyz were one as a people:
Not divided between north and south.
These nomads lived side by side
And shared a common soul.

538.

Alymbek was invited to Pishpek Castle,
Where blue bloods and aristocrats
Placed a crown upon his head
Saying he should be Khan of the Kyrgyz nation.

539.

If Alymbek asked for Russian help to crush Kokand
They would aid him gladly;
'But, Russia never considered the Kyrgyz
As equals and independent,' he reasoned.

540.

If I ask for weapons to take Kokand,
They will not reject my request.
But, Russia has its own language and spiritual values,
So, there can be no union between us.

541.

The Russians had established their power
In the region of Issyk-Kul,
Whilst others sided with Kokand.
How could the Kyrgyz people ever be joined together?

542.

Solto Biy, Abdylda Biy, Sultan Biy and all the blue bloods of
Jantay, the first families of Sarbagysh,
Wanting to protect the nation from aggressors
Gathered at Kastek Castle.

543.

Yet, how could these nomadic people
Establish a government for the whole nation?
However, the great aim of Alymbek to govern
Stayed but a dream despite his efforts.

544.

The throne of the Kókand by this time
Belonged to Shah Murad;
The fifteen-year-old reinstating
Alymbek as his vizier.

545.

Khudayar was furious that
Shah Murad had ascended to the throne
And promised pots of gold and silver
To the one who would bring him Alymbek's head.

546.

Though Alymbek Datka was blameless, conspirators whispered
Evil rumours about him to Shah Murad.
Betrayal surrounded Alymbek
And his closest friends were put to the sword.

547.

The palace was filled with intrigues,
Several attempts were made on Alymbek's life.
Therefore, he prepared to leave for Alay.
To consult with Kurmanjan.

548.

Kurmanjan was wise and told him,
'Don't go to the Khan's palace, my Bek.
There are too many enemies at hand,
With some lurking in the shadows.'

549.

'But I must visit the Khan,' he said,
How could I dare to ignore his orders?'
'Yet, I ask you not to go,' she replied,
'Because I foresee grave danger.'

550.

'My dear, you are my better half,' he uttered,
'But if ill-fortune awaits, let me meet it.
Indeed, don't dwell on ill-portents
And let me say goodbye to our children.'

551.

Deceived by plotters, Shah Murad believed
Alymbek to be an enemy of the Khanate,
And upon his arrival at the palace
Served upon him the sentence of death.

552.

They severed his head, while the walls ran red
With the blood of this hero, Alymbek.
His eyes remained open as his head rolled about
On the stone floor of the palace.

553.

When the head stopped rolling,
The killers took it in their hands,
Wrapped the body in linen
And took his corpse to the grave.

554.

It was a great tragedy for the Kyrgyz nation,
The sky cried and black fog covered the land.
The people had lost their hero like a lion:
Five sons, two daughters and a widow wept.

555.

Thunder ravaged the world:
An earthquake struck, which lasted for three days.
All the buildings were destroyed;
Since, Alymbek had died for no reason.

556.

It was in the year of 1862,
That Kurmanjan became a widow.
She'd foreseen it all in her vision,
Although feeling her grief would be endless.

557.

'I have lost my mighty lion,' she lamented,
'There will never be another such as him.
And his plan to establish Kyrgyz statehood
Is left behind as a dream unfulfilled.

558.

'You were the best warrior and leader,
You who loved your motherland
And defended it with your life.
If God allows, we will pursue the freedom you sought.'

559.

Being tolerant, Alymbek's sons
Followed in their Father's footsteps:
Praying to God and reading the Kuran,
While asking that his soul dwell in paradise.

MOURNING SONG

560.

'You were my honey, my darling,
And your body lies in Kokand.
I should like to plant trees by your grave
And make it an evergreen place.'

561.

'I will miss you, my honey, my darling,
I will miss the way your golden belt sparkled.
I should like to plant flowers by your grave
And make it into an eternal orchard.'

562.

'I will miss you, my honey, my darling,
I will miss the way your golden belt sparkled,
But now my lion is gone
And here no more.'

563.

'Your place was the Khan's palace,
You were the chief, the vizier.
You lived in Andijan and Kokand,
But, you were the Datka of our land.'

564.

'You were an adviser to many Khans,
And a good friend to the people.
You gave clarity to many Khans,
You were a warrior for our nation.'

565.

'Your horse was fleet of foot,
Your intelligence matched your horse.
Your horse was beautiful to behold,
Your manners matched your horse.'

566.

'Yet, I should not grieve,
Your grave will be a flowerbed;
Still, I should not grieve,
For you now reside in paradise.'

THE HARDSHIP OF LONELINESS

567.

Wearing a black hat,
Kurmanjan took care of her children,
She was sad but tried to lighten the mood of the palace.
Obviously, the forty tribes came to pay their respects.

568.

When Alymbek was alive,
Kurmanjan had administered the affairs of Alay.
She always made fair decisions,
Becoming a respected stateswoman!

569.

Kurmanjan was close to Mallya Beg's mother
Nadira, and they often consulted together
On policy within the palace
Or the problems facing the nation.

570.

With the position of Khan open once more,
The Bukharan Emir Muzaffar's troops arrived,
Surrounding thereby the Kokand Khanate
And nominating Khudayar for a new term.

571.

The Bukharan Emir came to Osh,
Where Kurmanjan met with him cordially.
He wanted to collaborate with the Kyrgyz nation, he said!
He'd come to award her the title of Datka.

572.

Kurmanjan asked that the title be given to Jarkymbai,
Who was the mayor of Osh at that time.
By refusing the title herself,
She suggested Jarkymbai was a hero.

573.

The blue bloods, Alymbek's relatives,
Yet, the heads of the tribes insisted it be her.
She was the only one who was worthy,
Although it was rare for a woman to be given such power.

574.

The Bukharan Emir and the Khan of Kokand
Supported the decision of the Kyrgyz nation,
Bestowing thereby this title upon her:
Her authority rising ever higher.

575.

Though she was still in mourning
For the loss of Alymbek Datka,
Her country, sons and daughters like orphans,
And the nation itself was honoured by this accolade.

576.

The title 'Datka' is of Bukharan origin,
With a meaning akin to 'wise General.'
Whoever receives such a distinction was considered
A religious leader in the vilayet too.
Indeed, those with complaints came to the Datka,
Who based their rulings on the Holy Kuran.

577.

The title of Datka was awarded to ten people
And came with a stipend:
Of one thousand coins
And two hundred sheaves of wheat a year.

578.

Compared with the other women of Asia,
Kyrgyz women were open-minded.
Kurmanjan was a fair judge,
And the nation loved her as their leader.

579.

The award of the title Datka to Kurmanjan
Was an important historic event.
'Widen the Silk Road,' Muzaffar told her,
'Let us make people's journeys more pleasant.'

580.

Alimqul occupied the throne in Kokand as regent
After Khudayar was once more driven out.
Mallya Beg's son, a twelve-year-old Sultan,
Was now the titular Khan.

581.

The leader of the Kyrgyz and the Kipchaks,
When Alimqul took power in his hands:
The position of the Khanate was weak,
With Russia ready to occupy Central Asia.

582.

It was the year of 1863,
And battles for the throne still raged:
Indeed, the Bukharan Emir wanted to bring back
Khudayar for a third time.

583.

The Bukharan Emir came to Osh with his army:
Alimqul had taxed his people harshly,
Even levying a tax on unborn children,
But, the coffers of the Khanate remained empty.

584.

With the power of the Khanate weakening,
And the unity of the palace broken,
With Khans changing regularly, one after another,
The Russian Empire found the land ripe for plunder.

585.

It was the year of 1865,
The Russian Empire's position grew stronger,
They occupied the north of the Kyrgyz lands,
Syr-Darya and Jety-Suu were under a Russian yoke.

586.

In the year of 1867, by the decree of Emperor Alexander II,
Konstantin Petrovich von Kaufman was named
The first Governor-General of Russian Turkestan
With fallen Tashkent as its capital.

587.

Districts were divided into regions
With Russian pickings at their heads.
Khudayar was returned as Khan for the fourth time,
But, had no true authority.

588.

People could find no money to pay taxes
So, Khudayar Khan growing crueller and weaker,
Allowed a tax to be levied on grass,
While those who couldn't pay were killed.

STRIKING OUT AGAINST THE KHAN

589.

People were tired of being exploited
And longed for their freedom.
Those from Ferghana (united under Iskhak Khasan's banner)
Were ready to fight against Khudayar Khan.

590.

Having failed to persuade Pulat Khan,
The grandson of Alim Khan to lead the uprising,
Khasan took on his epithet whereas in the sacred place of
Safed-Bulan, he sat upon the white felt.

591.

Khudayar sent warriors to punish
The followers on the false Khan,
But, this angered the mountain people,
Who struck against the Khudayar's soldiers!

592.

Abdrahman seemed to understand the people
And heard their complaints saying he would help.
He invited all the blue bloods to the palace
For an audience with the Khan.

593.

Let the Datkas come to the palace,
Let them give voice to the people's words.
Believing in him, the chiefs arrived:
The heads of the forty tribes.

594.

Torturing them like beasts, Khudayar had them executed;
The heads of the tribes among them.
Hearing of the Khan's insolence,
Those in the Ferghana Valley erupted.

595.

Hordes of angry Kyrgyz and Kipchak warriors
Began to vandalise the castles of Kokand.
In order to stop their revolt,
Beks arrived with their legions.

596.

The mountain people showed their might,
And drove out the Beks.
They occupied Osh and Kurgan:
They occupied Andijan and Bulak Bashy.

597.

On the banks of the turbulent Naryn River,
Lost in the middle of the great valley,
The hunter, Mamyr was the head of his people,
Though he came from an ordinary family.

598.

The people's rebel Mamyr came to Kok-Art:
Capturing Jalal-Abad, Khanabad and Uzgen in July.
Despite their brave resistance, though,
The Khan's troops crushed their uprising.

599.

Mamyr led the rebels in Leilek,
But, Abdrahman was sent to suppress them.
Four hundred people were captured
And driven to Kokand to be hanged.

600.

The uprising lasted for three long years,
Families numbering 132,000 from forty-two clans
Took part in the rebellion
Against the Khan's ruthless exploitation.

601.

Pulat Khan came to Leilek,
To become leader of the uprising.
Indeed, his vast influence over all
Left the Khan confused and conflicted.

602.

Khudayar put forward his son Nasruddin.
It was high time to select a new Khan,
Going against Abdrahman and others
Who opposed this continuance.

603.

Khudayar fled to Russia,
And Nasruddin was named the new Khan.
Pulat Khan was captured and jailed,
But, he soon escaped.

604.

Nasruddin wanted to drive out
The Russian invaders, but
Governor-General Kaufman
Drafted in five thousand soldiers.

605.

With the Khanate once again awash with blood,
Nasruddin met with Kaufman.
He was forced to sign documents abolishing the Khanate
And annex the land to the Ferghana Oblast.

606.

Skobelev was appointed first military Governor of Ferghana.
His men soon opening fire on an unarmed crowd,
So, Abdrahman met with Pulat Khan
To draw up a plan to drive out the Russians.

607.

On the 20th of September 1895, Pulat Khan overthrew
Nasruddin and vowed to turn his army against Russia.
So, twenty thousand died! Skobelev's diaries from that time
Stating 'peace and order in Asia directly relates to the number
of massacred people and their dismembered heads.'

608.

Pulat Khan was imprisoned in February 1896,
While the fight for freedom was lost.
Vowing vengeance, Skobelev had
Pulat Khan hanged in public.

609.

Many perished in the cold revolution
Against this colonial yoke.
Yet, their heroism endures in the pages of history:
Their noble deeds recounted.

ABDYLDABEK'S FATE

610.

Abdyldabek, the son of noble Kurmanjan and Alymbek
Was against Russian rule.
So, when the revolt against Khudayar Khan begun,
Kurmanjan blessed her son and told him, 'Save your nation.'

611.

Even in the darkest moments,
He pursued his Father's belief in freedom,
And by his close friend, Pulat Khan
Was appointed a position of importance.

612.

It was in the year of 1876,
When the Khanate had been dissolved,
That Abdyldabek hoisted the Kyrgyz flag on Jaman-Too
And vowed to expel the colonialists.

613.

Abdyldabek and Omorbek raised an army of fifteen hundred,
And constructed fortifications in the hills of Alay.
They may not have had weapons like the Russians,
But, their spirits were indomitable.

614.

The Russians wanted to cement their power
In the Ferghana Valley.
So, on the 25th of April, Skobelev arrived
To wage war against the Kyrgyz nation.

615.

The battle lasted for two days,
Yet, the Kyrgyz were outgunned.
Abdyldabek's forces retreated to the mountains,
To take up guerilla tactics.

616.

Throughout summer the uprising spread:
Villagers uniting in the struggle.
However, to crush their dreams, Skobelev
Vowed to kill Abdyldabek.

617.

On the invitation of the Russian General,
Shabdan-Baatyr came to Alay,
His mediation in the conflict
Preventing much bloodshed.

618.

The struggle for independence
Rumbled on for two years;
The Russians didn't know
How to subdue it.

619.

Skobelev wrote to the heads of the tribes
Saying the Emperor had asked him to bring peace to the area,
Although those who continued to help the resistance
Would be severely punished!

620.

'If you bring Abdyldabek to me
Dead or alive,' he wrote,
'You will win the
Favour of the Empire.'

621.

Skobelev wrote to Abdyldabek
A letter hand-delivered by Abdrahman
Saying he would be vanquished,
If he did not lay down his arms.

622.

'You used Nasruddin as a puppet,'
Abdyldabek replied, 'then
Sent him to jail in Siberia.
I am against such deception.'

623.

'Your Excellency, dear General Skobelev,
You promised to leave our biys in Kokand
Like our dear Abdrahman.
But, you sent them to jail in Siberia,
So, how can we trust your words?'

624.

'This is why the Kyrgyz and Kipchaks revolt,
You promised to be our friend, then deceived us.
How can we believe you
When you break your solemn oaths?'

625.

'You only trust force, but we place our faith in Allah:
Nomadic people value freedom above all else.
If you will let Shabdan rule the land, we will stop the revolt,
If not, we will resist you until our dying breaths.'

626.

This letter is still kept in a respected archive
So, these words will never be forgotten:
Penned by Abdyldabek's hand,
It is dated and marked with his seal.

627.

Abdyldabek went to Kyzylart and gathered his soldiers,
Deciding to leave for Afghanistan, so that they may regroup.
Travelling with two of his brothers, he crossed the pass,
Determined to return and fight once more.

628.

Harried by bandits along the way,
It took time to arrive in Afghanistan.
Nobody knew what fate would befall him.
Yet, finally succeeding, Abdyldabek
Presented his horse to the Afghan Khan.

629.

When the Khan saw his dishevelled state, he said,
'You are sick and tired, but as a Datka, I greet you cordially
And respect your action in presenting to me this fine horse.
However, my friend, you should keep your gift
To ride on a pilgrimage with me to Mecca and Madina.'

630.

Illness overcame Abdyldabek; his health deteriorated.
He said to his brothers, 'don't leave my body
In this foreign land, take me back to Alay.'
Clearly, Abdyldabek would never see his native land again:
Never lay eyes on the Ala-Too Mountains.

BRINGING ABDYLDABEK'S BODY BACK TO ALAY

631.

Asanbek and Mamatbek crossed the mountains
Encountering hardships as they carried their brother,
But, Abdyldabek's wish to fulfil his Father's dream
Was destined to perish in Afghanistan.

632.

When his heart stopped beating,
His brother's cries of anguish
Reverberated through the mountains.
They travelled on for three months
To return Abdyldabek to his motherland.

633.

'Let them bury my bones according to Muslim rules,'
He'd told his brothers.
'Let the people know I died without fear
Whilst trying to make my father's dream a reality.'

KURMANJAN'S MOURNING SONG FOR HER SON

634.

'Oh, my dear son, you added relish to my life,
Oh, my dear son, your passing is a torment to me.
Oh, my darling, it is a bitter pill;
I will miss you as long as I live.'

635.

'From the high pass why didn't you emerge
To greet me, my son?
I feel as if my heart has been ripped out,
A sword shorn through my liver.'

636.

'Why couldn't you return to Alay
Upon your steed, my dear?
The freedom for which you pined
Wasn't destined for your proud nation.'

637.

'Why couldn't you return to Alay
Upon your fine grey mount?
The freedom that you sought
Wasn't destined for your proud nation.'

638.

'You died for no reason, my dear son;
May your soul reside in paradise.
Oh, my dear firstborn child,
May your soul reside in paradise.'

THE PASSAGE OF THE REVOLT AFTER ABDYLDABEK'S DEPARTURE TO AFGHANISTAN

639.

Supporting Abdyldabek's ideas,
The mountain people continued their uprising.
Without fear of death, they planned to fight,
And let Russian soldiers learn of Kyrgyz courage.

640.

The people of the Sokh River were ready to revolt:
Mambet-Biy, Kudainazar, Jarmamabet,
Mamatkerim, Muratbai and Eshmambet
Joined with Ashyr's army.

641.

With the Russians on the offensive.
The Holy man, Ashyr decided to save his head
And flee to Kara-Tegin,
Yet, he was captured en route.

642.

Kurmanjan was set to leave for Afghanistan,
But, Skobelev asked for an audience and she agreed to meet.
Accompanied by her retinue:
Her grandson, Myrzapayaz among them,
Her son, Kamchybek, heading the procession
To take care of her security.

643.

They arrived at Archa Bulak,
Where Skobelev's camp was on the highway.
Russian soldiers helped her from her horse,
Addressing her politely as the Queen of the Mountains.

644.

When Skobelev greeted her for the first time,
Kurmanjan was in the position of the defeated party.
Yet, she conducted herself like a queen for her nation,
Making decisions and taking notes on the meeting.

645.

Kurmanjan was wise and saw the futility of continued resistance:
She'd sign the document of annexation, she said,
If Skobelev would sincerely guarantee
That the land would be at peace.

646.

'I ask you to keep peace in our nation,' she said,
'Let people live full lives.
If you fulfil this promise and make no false declaration,
I will cooperate with all of my heart.'

647.

She'd accept the suzerainty of Russia
And agree that their lands be united.
She'd foreseen that this was the only
Possible outcome for some time.

648.

As a mark of his respect to her,
Governor-General Skobelev
Presented her a coat of silver threads
And a golden cup.

649.

She was agonised by the predicament,
But she didn't want her people's blood spilt.
It was better to be united with Russia,
She'd announce before the nation.

650.

'Oh, my nation,' she declared, 'please, listen to my order.
We are to be united with this Russian power.
I call on you to live in peace,
To live in unity.'

651.

Kurmanjan was angry and upset,
That as of this time she'd had no word from
Her three sons in Afghanistan.
She thought about her sons who were lost
And the perils facing them in the form of Russians.
She thought a thousand times about the fate of the nation,
And her aim to keep her people from death's clutches.

652.

It was in the year of 1876, that the Kyrgyz
Of the south ended their war with Russia.
Alay, Gulcha, Ak-Buura, Nookat and Uzgen
Now belonged to the Great Empire.

653.

In the year of 1877,
When Mamatbek and Asanbek returned
They began to rule over Osh, Uzgen, Nookat and Alay.
They accepted the annexation and came to the decision
That it was better to live in peace.

654.

Omorbek ruled in Gulcha,
Fulfilling his duties honestly.
He was as respected as his ancestors,
A true son of the motherland.

655.

Beloved by the people, Asanbek ruled in Nookat,
But, the Russians sent him to jail
In the province of Irkutsk, where Mamatbek was also
Imprisoned despite promises regarding his liberty.

656.

Kamchybek ruled in Alay.
Her youngest son, the apple of his mother's eye
Resolving the problems of his people
And becoming dear to them.

KAMCHYBEK'S DILEMMA

657.

Kamchybek and his wife Asel,
Were coming from Kashgar with items for the household:
Through the border area of Erkeshtam
Where caravans passed on the Silk Road.

658.

The head of the caravan was Akpalvan:
They were stopped by customs officers,
Who treated them barbarically,
Saying they were carrying prohibited goods.

659.

The inspectors of the customs office,
Demanded they open their packages,
Yet, as her case required a key.
Asel refused to hand it over.

660.

The Russian soldiers pulled Asel down by her hair and cut it:
A great shame in Kyrgyz culture.
According to long-held traditions
A virtuous woman's hair should remain uncut.

661.

Because they cut Asel's hair,
Local Kyrgyz warriors were outraged.
Because they cut Asel's hair,
These warriors with a strong belief in tradition
Fought with these Russian soldiers.
Three officers were killed.
Whereas they buried their bodies in a ravine.
It was Akpalvan's order to do so.

662.

The military court held for Akpalvan
Passed a sentence of death.
Kamchybek was also to be punished
As if he led a criminal gang.
Obviously, the people were incensed,
And an undercurrent of revolt brew for good reason.

663.

Kurmanjan didn't know what to do
And couldn't sleep at night;
If they rose up against the Russians,
There would a bloody war.

664.

They had enough forces to fight,
But the Russians were well-equipped.
She had to support her son, though,
Hence, Kurmanjan could see no way out.

665.

As her grandchildren, Myrzapayaz and Arstanbek
Were with the party, they would also be punished.
Indeed, by special order of the Russian military court,
They were sent to jail in Siberia.

666.

It was March 2nd, 1895,
A beautiful spring day, when
Kurmanjan's life turned to winter.
By an unfair decision of the Russian court,
Her son, Kamchybek was to be hung before her eyes:
Such was the cruelty of the Russian Emperor.

667.

Her sons, Mamatbek and Asanbek,
Were additionally sent to the province of Irkutsk:
In the Taishet gulag there,
They would know only ill-fortune.

668.

Kamchybek did not deserve his fate,
Yet, the Russians suspected the family of harbouring
Their Father's ambitions.
They planned to commit genocide on Alymbek's tribe,
They planned to kill Alymbek's younger brother: Jarkymbai,
Abdyldabek had also fallen. Now planning to kill Mamatbek,
Even her grandson, Myrzapayaz, was no longer safe.

669.

Kurmanjan's grandson, Arstanbek
Was not even an adult: he was just thirteen.
But, they sent him to the dark forests of Siberia
To labour in a gulag.

670.

Kurmanjan suffered greatly,
Whilst these events are recorded in historic annals.
Yet, this Queen without a crown or throne,
Negotiated with generals for the good of her nation.

671.

Her clear skies covered by black smoke,
Fortune didn't smile upon her,
But to save the peace of her people,
She wore the black headdress of mourning.

672.

Ruling that Kamchybek had killed the customs officers,
Without analysing any facts, the Russians hanged her son
Before her eyes. Obviously, she knew if she protested
They'd use this pretext to annihilate the Kyrgyz nation.

KURMANJAN DATKA'S LAMENT

673.

'Though you stared them down, as strong as a lion,
They hung you right before my eyes.
So, my heart is aflame with indignation,
And its black smoke spreads across the sky.'

674.

'My heart is burning, an open fire.
Its smoke carrying laments to the highest firmament.
Now raven clouds cover my days,
While the Sky cries out with regret.'

675.

'My sorrow is incurable,
My pain cannot be extinguished.
No longer among the stars in the sky,
Kamchybek's light has been extinguished.'

676.

‘You, my dear son, were a part of my body,
No mother should live to see their child die.
“Look at death without fear,” I told you,
Though my heart was broken and bleeding.’

677.

‘A woman at home, but an eagle in public.
I saved my nation and kept the peace,
But, I lost my son, as brave as a lion,
And now my soul is tormented.’

678.

‘My objective was to keep my nation at peace,
But now, I am like a horse who has lost its colt.
Even though I remain alive as a leader,
Inside I am dead.’

679.

‘I try to remain strong in spirit and body,
But, I sacrificed myself for the nation.
Although you were ready to die for our motherland,
I mourn your loss as a mother.’

680.

‘As a mother, I sang you lullabies,
But now, my nights are empty and sleepless.
In private, I light candles for you,
But in public, I can never express my grief.’

681.

‘I weep for my little colt as a mother
Who couldn’t stop the cruel Russians.
I watched you hang steely-eyed, though crying inside,
But you were right to die standing rather than be a slave.’

682.

‘Though your sentence was wholly unjust,
What can be dearer than the fortune of our nation?
If we had fought for your life to be saved,
The enemy would have killed us all.’

683.

‘Though I agreed you must meet your fate,
Please, don’t think me a cruel mother.
My heart died twice when at first the rope broke,
Then they hung you for a second time.’

684.

'All the people of Alay gathered for your execution
While their hearts died with you.
When the rope broke I said fate wanted you to live,
But the murderers didn't listen to my words.'

685.

'The pages of history will record
That your punishment was unwarranted,
But they will equally remember you as a hero
Who met his end bravely for our motherland.'

686.

'Driven to despair, the Alay Queen weeps silently,
Since no mother should outlive her children,
But, let other children of our nation be safe
And not be lost to these flames that devour me.'

KURMANJAN'S MOURNING SONG FOR HER SON, KAMCHYBEK

687.

'I lost my leonine son;
Only death can save me from this torment.
I wear a blue dress
As a sign of my hidden mourning.

688.

'You met death without fear
But grief twists inside me like a snake
Because I couldn't save you, my son,
Because I couldn't beg for your life.'

689.

'Let the mountain flowers never fade,
Let nobody else die as young as you;
May God punish the Russians
Who slew you for no reason.'

690.

'Let the valleys bloom not fade,
Let nobody else die young like you;
Those who hung you for no reason,
Let them face capital punishment.'

691.

‘I am the Datka of the nation,
This is why they took your life, my dear,
My enemies wanted to see my tears,
But I’ll never give them the satisfaction.’

692.

‘Though you lived a short life,
You saved our nation from annihilation;
Farewell, my darling, my honey,
May you find a home in paradise.’

ADDRESSING DEATH

693.

‘Oh, Lord, let me die instead of my children.
Or burn me alive, but why must you punish me?
I would rather live in hell than see my children pass;
Oh, Lord, please let them live.’

694.

‘I gave my baby into death’s clutches:
He was sent to a world without sin.
Why did you torture me, delivering me to the abyss
By hanging my child before my eyes?’

695.

‘Don’t come, cruel death, don’t cross the mountains,
Don’t come, let life be eternal.
Don’t come, cruel death, don’t take my baby
Who had just begun to live.’

696.

‘Oh, God, don’t make me grieve,
Don’t send death, I beg of you.
Don’t take my strong son to the next world.
Let death disappear like clouds in the sky.’

KURMANJAN DATKA, POLITICIAN AND STATESWOMAN

697.

It was the year 1876 –
The life of Kurmanjan Datka passed in this way.
The Russians ruled with an iron fist,
But, Kurmanjan guided her nation along the right path.

698.

Though her power was limited under the Russians,
Kurmanjan saved her nation as a Mother to her people.
Though Ferghana was ruled by a Governor-General,
Kurmanjan was the true Queen of the Alay.

699.

Famous people throughout the Russian Empire
Saw their respects for Kurmanjan multiply:
Even the Governor-General of Turkestan
Referred to her as Queen of the Alay.

700.

When Russian power came to pass,
Kurmanjan had to leave her palace in Gulcha,
Indeed, when visiting on official business,
She lived in Alymbek's homestead in Alay.

701.

Kurmanjan often visited Osh
To speak to the people about their lives.
She spent the winters in Mady,
While the rest of the year in Gulcha.

702.

Kurmanjan was known to all of the governors
As a wise politician and stateswoman.
All the governors treated her with deference,
Inviting her to summits and gatherings.

703.

As Governor-General of Russian Turkestan,
Kaufman met with Kurmanjan in Mady on official business.
He asked her to collaborate with the Tsar's guidance,
And she agreed, saying 'for the sake of peace.'

704.

In the year of 1884,
A great summit was held in Margalang,
Wherein Kurmanjan signed a peace accord with
Rozenbakh, the new Governer-General of Russian Turkestan.

705.

As a sign of his respect, the Governor-General
Presented Kurmanjan with a gold brocade:
Governors from around the Empire came
To Alay and Osh to consult with her and seek her advice.

706.

Kurmanjan helped raise funds to
Build the Gulcha-Taldyk-Erkeshtam Highway
By collecting 25,000 Som. She explained to her people
The benefits the road would bring.
Clearly, the black fog of loss still obscured the blue sky,
Yet, only Kurmanjan could have persuaded them at this time.

707.

In the year of 1897,
Mamatbek was released from the gulag.
Later that same year, Myrzapayaz was set free,
Which heartened Kurmanjan gladly.

708.

In the year of 1898,
At a special summit in Osh, Kurmanjan met with
Dukhovsky, the next Governer-General of Russian Turkestan,
To discuss the political situation and the future of the realm.

709.

Kurmanjan was almost ninety at the time,
But, her intelligence remained undiminished.
Dukhovsky admired her, saying, 'I can see you
Wanted unending peace and prosperity for your nation.'

710.

She received eight different Governor-Generals in her home,
As attested by history books;
Indeed, by decree of the Emperor,
She was even supported with a pension.

711.

As the first stateswoman of Central Asia,
The Kyrgyz people still revere Kurmanjan.
Hence, awarded the Andreev medal by the Russians,
Her refusal of this prize remains unknown.

712.

In recognition of her years of service, Emperor Alexander II
Sent Kurmanjan a brilliant ring:
Some of her correspondence with these authorities survive
And were kept in a box by her son Mamatbek!

713.

Datka's sage words still honour the nation,
Which she saw through a period of chaotic transition.
The Kyrgyz saw Russians as their enemies;
While a song meant to frighten children contains
The words, 'the Russians are coming.'

714.

'Let us not be at war,' Kurmanjan said,
Even though the Russians had killed members of her family
And others sent to Siberia.
Certainly, she wanted the freedom her husband had
Strived for, but instead kept the nation from genocide.

715.

Kyrgyz, Kipchak, Uzbek, Tajik or Kazakh,
She treated all as equals.
As a result, her fame spread,
She was known in China, Iran and Afghanistan.

716.

Guillaume Capus, the French ethnologist and
His countryman, the explorer Gabriel Bonvalot
Met with Kurmanjan. They explained their goal was
Travelling overland to India, whereby Kurmanjan's children
Helped them cross the Pamir. Certainly, they wrote
This was the 'roof of the world.'

717.

'She has a special quality,' Capros wrote of Kurmanjan.
'She is greatly respected in her community
And throughout the nation.
There is something about her which touches people.'

718.

'The way she values all is
Truly a wonderful quality.
She is the finest diplomat in this land,
Which is occupied by Russians.'

719.

British spies arrived in the land. The Great Game was afoot.
So, knowing these facts, she dared not antagonise Russia,
Although she rebuffed their advances.
Nevertheless, they wrote she was 'a natural diplomat.'

AGAIN, UNREST

720.

In the year of 1898,
Local people gathered in the spring.
They were against Russian occupation, they said.
There was unrest in Andijan and Kokand.

721.

They had a great meeting to outline their demands.
The people brought the famous
Dukchi Eshen, Muhammad Ali Madali
To be their leader.

722.

It was their duty to involve not only the people
Of Ferghana, but also those from the whole of the south.
They must propagate their vision,
And to do this they enlisted the ideologue, Mullah Ziyadin.

723.

A son of the Tolos tribe, Ziyadin
Had served the Khans of Kokand in his time.
He was famous in Central Asia and Russia,
And had written a history of Andijan.

724.

Madali thought they were sure to win;
With people from Ketmen Tobo, Kuba,
Uzgen, Osh, Nookat, Asake and Margalang,
They were sure to beat the Russians this time.

725.

In order to win freedom for the people,
Madali gathered two thousand warriors.
They attacked the garrison in Andijan
Killing twenty two Russian soldiers.

726.

It was all over within a week, however,
The Russians executed eighteen participants
Whilst another 356 were sent to Siberia
For their part in the uprising.

727.

The Russians focused their vengeance on the village
Of Kok-Art, where Madali was born:
Razing it to the ground
Where it lay in ashes.

728.

The homes of a thousand people were destroyed
And they were left destitute to starve.
It is written in scripts from that era
How the Kyrgyz people would never forget this insult.

729.

The people of Alay were ready to rise up,
But knowing the Russians were well-armed,
Kurmanjan dissuaded them:
Her actions saved their lives.

730.

'I can foresee how events will unfold,'
She told them, 'If we attack the Russians,
Shouting out our battle cry,
Will only lead to bloodshed for our people.'

731.

Back in the year of 1850,
Alymbek had built a madrassa in the city of Osh.
People were satisfied with his great endeavour,
You can read about his educative work in the archives of Osh.

732.

In the spirit of her late husband,
Kurmanjan built the first school
To educate the children of the Alay region
And teach them Arabic script.

733.

Up until the 1960s,
That first madrassa built by Kurmanjan
Was a centre of education:
Even though it was converted to a storehouse.

734.

In the year of 1906,
At the age of ninety five,
Kurmanjan visited mountain pastures to drink
Fresh mare's milk, saamal, and to rest.

735.

Baron Carl Gustaf Emil Mannerheim,
A Russian secret intelligence officer
Travelling as an ethnographer
Even went to Alay to meet her.

736.

A Finnish citizen, Mannerheim
Later became a colonel in the Russian Army.
In 1944, he became famous
As the President of Finland.

737.

He came to Alay on a mission to search for
British and Japanese spies and to gauge
Local attitudes to the Han Chinese.
He later wrote a book about his travels.

738.

It was prohibited at that time as a sin
Under Islam to have photographs taken,
But, in her old age, Kurmanjan consented,
And Mannerheim's shots recorded her for posterity.

739.

Though she was ninety five,
Mannerheim wanted to take a picture
Of Kurmanjan on a horse: where she sat,
Beautifully adorned with her grandson beside her.

740.

She had always ridden masterfully,
Leaving troubles and tortures to the wind,
Albeit there she sat, captured in these photographs,
As a phenomenon, the Queen of the Alay.

741.

It is an everlasting story, never to be repeated;
That Governer-General Dukhovsky's wife,
Princess Barbara, wrote of her meeting with Kurmanjan
By saying she had the grace of Classical Cornelia.

742.

Princess Barbara Dukhovskya-Golitsyn
Wrote of the Queen of the Alay
With admiration for her charm and wisdom:
Noting how refined she was.

743.

Janybek was a wise judge
And Kurmanjan's trusted confidant;
Balkyn was his sister,
Whilst Omor advised Janybek as a close friend.

744.

When Janybek organised an event in Kara-Shoro
In remembrance of his father, he invited Datka
As a venerable guest; he wanted to secure her blessings
nd ordered the village made ready.

745.

Despite her advanced years, Kurmanjan came on a stallion
With her grandchild accompanying her:
Through meadows rich with fragrance,
She arrived in the village of Kakyr.

746.

Eager to greet Datka, Janybek met her along the way.
In Kakyr, where she had stopped to rest and eat.
Janybek requested the people come to Kakyr.
Instead, Kara-Shoko said 'erect a national house for her:
The Mother of our Nation must be made comfortable.'

747.

Everybody welcomed her when they arrived,
Paying great attention to her every step.
A bear-skin rug was placed under her:
ll the ladies greeting her with deference.

748.

The place where Janybek held a ceremony for his Father
Is still known as 'Kurmanjan's Place' to this day.
It is considered sacred even now
Whereas people still travel there to pay their respects.

The Gathering

749.

The poem of Kurmanjan's life is everlasting,
As was the fount of her wisdom.
The story is not finished, even now
If researching her name and her deeds.

750.

Kurmanjan received guests from Turkestan, Russia and Europe,
And treated them with famed Kyrgyz hospitality.
Indeed, many wrote of her in their memoirs,
And recalled her kindness and sincerity.

751.

Traditions were observed to respect guests:
Elders were treated with special esteem.
Men were always seated on the left,
While women on the right.

752.

The table brimmed with fresh fruit and vegetables:
Tea was readied in a samovar.
Young ladies served them with dignity,
To those who came from far and wide.

753.

You couldn't help but admire the generous spread:
Boorsoq fried in butter, naan, qattama,
Lavash, kurut balls, rice and wheat porridge
Of which many guests wrote.

754.

There was hand-milled popped corn to snack upon,
And maksym and jarma to quench thirsts.
As children waited for the corn to pop,
They would gather around the oven to warm their hands.

755.

Kurmanjan made a special drink of butter and honey,
Which children never forgot to taste.
It became a speciality that
Still exists in modern times.

756.

Kurmanjan was a master of all trades. She made horse tack and
Embroidered her granddaughter's dowries.
She handcrafted carpets, weaving the threads,
Now housed in museums, with their qualities undiminished.

TOLERANCE

757.

Her sons, as their father had done, looked like lions,
Protecting the nation and receiving its blessings;
Her daughters were charming and elegant
And displayed the wisdom they had inherited.

758.

Abdyldabek worked in positions his father had held;
In the fight for independence alongside Pulat Khan,
He was the leader of their war staff, working exactingly:
He was briefly vizier of the Kokand Khanate.

759.

Omorbek fought for independence,
Against the occupiers.
During the Russian colonial period,
Mamatbek served as Governor of Bulak Bashy.

760.

Alymbek's younger brother, Jarkymbay
Was like a son to Kurmanjan,
But alas, the brave warrior fell in battle
Against Governor-General Chernyayav near Tashkent.

761.

It was on the 1st of February, 1907,
That Kurmanjan left this world.
Thousands came to her funeral,
The whole nation was stricken with grief.

762.

She was buried with great ceremony,
In Sar-Mazar, not far from Osh,
Where her youngest son, Kamchybek's, body laid;
May she rest with him forever!

763.

In the newspapers of Turkestan,
Having considered the mood of the nation,
The authorities of the Russian Empire
Wrote to express their condolences.

764.

Yuvachev was the first to undertake research on Datka;
Though many died, her two sons survived her:
Two daughters, thirty-one grandchildren,
Fifty-seven great-grandchildren
And six great-great-grandchildren.

KURMANJAN'S BURIAL SONG AS SUNG BY HER GRANDCHILDREN

765.

'There is a wind on the top of the white rocks
But, death finds its way through regardless.
If only there would be no death,
And I could still be together with my ancestors.'

766.

'There is a wind on the mountain peaks,
But, sorrow finds its way through regardless.
If only there would be no death,
And I could still be together with my ancestors.'

767.

'You always wore your white elechek,
You raised the dearest children.
You were the Queen of the Alay,
Beloved by God and our nation.'

768.

'You were always hospitable, even to your enemies,
You had no crown or palace,
Though you were our Queen,
And leader of our Kyrgyz nation.'

769.

'You always wore your tall, white elechek,
And were often mounted on your fine stead.
Your aim was always to establish peace: you were
Beloved by God and our nation.'

770.

'Your golden bells jingled when you walked,
Bringing with you harmony.
You were charming, like the moon,
Enlightening our lives.'

771.

'You lived a long life until almost a hundred,
Your sons, daughters and their children
Will remember you for all of their days
And await your counsel in the next world.'

772.

'You supported us through thick and thin,
Yet, who will support us now?
When your life was extinguished, things became dark,
Yet, who will guide us now?'

773.

'In this mountainous place where the past echoes,
You lost your husband long ago,
But though a widow and alone,
You only grew stronger.'

774.

'In this rugged place where there is no way out,
You lost your babies long ago,
But, though you suffered greatly,
You sagely led us through the storms.'

775.

'You rode a grey horse across the mountains.
So, when travelers passed along the Silk Road
They admired your hospitality and humanity.
May you reside in paradise, my dear.'

776.

'The warmth of your house shone, like pearls,
Oh, Grandma, you were a close friend
Your soul was beautiful, like pearls,
Oh, Grandma, you were a close friend.'

777.

'You always had fine sugar for my tea.
This was a great pleasure for me.
But, only to speak with you
Was the greatest pleasure for my soul.'

778.

'You always had the best red tea.
This was a great pleasure for me,
But, only to speak with you
Was the greatest pleasure for my soul.'

779.

'You always had the best jarma,
But, where will we find it now?
You always had the best kumis of fine mare's milk,
But, where will we find it now Datka has gone?'

780.

'You were the pride of our nation,
Your sons the finest in the country.
Your home was built from the best birch wood,
Your daughters became real ladies.'

781.

'You shone like an amulet,
Yet, were the only one who took care of us.
You were the amulet around our necks,
Always protecting us.'

782.

'May you wear golden rings,
May you live in paradise.
May you wear silver rings,
May you live in paradise.'

783.

'Let's speak no more of our pain;
May you live in paradise.
Oh, let's speak no more of our troubles;
May you reside in paradise.'

THE FORTUNE OF DATKA'S ANCESTORS FROM THE SOVIET-ERATO MODERN TIMES

784.

During the Soviet-era, Kurmanjan's ancestors were tormented.
As the descendants of a titled family.
Indeed, they were labelled bourgeoisie, and many
Perished in jail.

785.

Things started auspiciously. Kurmanjan's grandchildren
Kamchybekov, Kadyrbek and Jamshytbek
Served in the Soviet Army as commanders
While even being awarded medals of distinction.

786.

In the year of 1937, though,
They were targeted as the ancestors of
A feudal power during Stalin's purges,
While one and all fell victim.

787.

In the jails of the NKVD, Abdyldabek's son
Myrzapayaz, felt the weight of oppression.
Musa Adyshev's father died in a camp,
Making Musa and his sister, Jama, orphans though only babes.

788.

An old man, Aidar, took care of them,
Working hard to raise them as if he were their father.
But, when Jama became the bride of a rich man from Kashgar
Without consent, Musa was sent to an orphanage.

789.

He stayed there until he finished school, then he went to fight
In the Great Patriotic War. He showed a lot of heroism,
Like his great-grandfather, Alymbek,
Before returning home in 1944 to Alay, safe and sound.

790.

Musa began to study and work in the
Institute of Geology, but he was often targeted
As an ancestor of Datka: a persecution enduring
On and off for the next twenty-five years.

791.

In a meeting of the Communist Party,
He was accused of deliberately concealing
His blue blood heritage and threatened with ejection
From the presidium of the Academy of Sciences.

792.

But there is the saying that ‘right will win out,’
And Musa succeeded regardless.
Specifically, he researched the ores of the region,
Certain developmental paths rested in natural resources.

793.

‘Yes, very rare metals in Kyrgyzstan,’ he reasoned,
‘Like vanadium, black shale, molybdenum and gold
Will provide for our Kyrgyz nation.’
While scientists have heeded his words ever since.

794.

The Head of the Kyrgyz SSR, Ishkak Razzakov,
When looking for young specialists, invited Musa
To come home and work in the sphere of the geology,
And so he returned from Tashkent.

795.

He worked in the Institute of Geology, rising through the ranks
To become President of the Kyrgyz Academy of Sciences, but
After only forty days in the position, in 1979, it was his fate
To pass into the next world.

796.

The Institute of Geology of the Kyrgyz Academy of Science
Is now named after Musa Adyshev.
The Osh Technological Institute
Now bears the name of Musa Abyshev.

797.

Musa's son, Janybek, lives in the United States,
He is now a professor, a scientist, researcher
And the author of more than fifty papers
On molecular biology, biomedical science and ecology.

798.

Kurmanjan's great-great-grandson, Chynybek, continues
To dream of the unity of the forty tribes,
With no more divisions
Between north and south.

799.

There is an old proverb which saying,
'If you break away from the group, a wolf can eat you
With no problem;' so, he works towards a congress
That will fulfil Alymbek's dream.

800.

Within our modern generation
We need more men like Alymbek
And more women like Kurmanjan
Who will follow our ancestor's directions.

801.

As for female descendants, Muratalieva Suusar
Is the very model of a Kyrgyz lady.
The head of a high school and an excellent teacher
She educates our nation.

802.

Another ancestor of our great Datkas,
Sarbanova Khandoolot, is a well-known doctor.
She contributes greatly to the health of our nation
As a specialist in combustiology.

803.

Omurzakova Tursunay, the great-granddaughter of
Kamchybek is a Director of Humanities
At the National Academy of Science:
A historian and scientist, she has published numerous books.

804.

Tursunay researched the activities of her ancestors,
And deeply studied archives in Moscow,
St. Petersburg, Osaka and Tashkent
To verify truth and legend.

805.

She routed out historical inaccuracies in
Remy-Dor's book, The Kyrgyz of the Afghan Pamir.
She was the inspiration
Behind my writing.

806.

The ancestors of our Kurmanjan Datka
Live in Kara-Suu, Uzgen, Osh and Alay;
They live in Chyi and Bishkek, and the United States,
Continuing their forebears' legacy.

ACTIVITIES DEVOTED TO KURMANJAN DATKA

807.

In the year of 1990,
We celebrated the 180th anniversary of the birth of Datka.
Guests arrived from around the world.
The words of prominent
Bards rose up and I vowed to pen my song.

808.

The greatest woman in Kyrgyz history,
Albeit too many years had passed
Before this celebration.
But, we should never forget her.

809.

Let us remember Kurmanjan's name,
Let's recall her deeds every day.
Let our country flourish and develop
Let happiness find us in every way.

ETERNAL HERITAGE

810.

Mother Datka left an eternal heritage.
She was wise and lived by example,
Even though she had no palace or crown.
She was Queen of the Alay.

811.

She put her stamp on the decree of friendship,
While being a stateswoman and a patriot.
A marvel from our nation
Written into the pages of global history.

812.

Although she endured great hardships,
Her tolerance and stamina were unrivalled.
Sometimes I have seen her in the dreams,
Since I started to write this poem.

813.

Her life was a shining example
Of bravery that never stumbles.
Future generations can still learn from her,
And her legacy will never die.

AFTERWORD

When I first wrote this poem about Kurmanjan Datka, I published some verses in a magazine. After that, I received a message from Mirlan Janybekov asking me to add some information he'd heard in a story told by his great-grandfather and great-grandmother.

— *Bubaisha Arstynbekova*

My great-grandfather's name was Omor. He was born in the Uzgen region in the township Ak-Jar of Osh county in the Ferghana Valley. He worked in the Uzgen region as a kazy – a judge. After the October Revolution, he was considered the ancestor of a bourgeoisie family and as a result, he fought for the Kyrgyz nation's freedom and was subsequently labelled a basmachi. Later they discovered that he was one of the best judges in that area, had served well and honestly and was worthy of his position. His name was Janybek.

Janybek hosted a great mourning ceremony to commemorate his father some time after his passing and invited Kurmanjan Datka to attend. On the way from Alay to Kara-Shoro, she wanted to rest and eat a little and they stopped in Kakyr. She got off her horse and sat on the ground for a while. As he was eager to meet her, Janybek was waiting along the way. Anyway, out of respect for her, he asked the people to erect a yurt in which she might rest. Janybek Kazy then requested that people come to Kakyr, where they would hold the mourning feast, instead of Kara-Shoro. It is a historical fact.

According to my grandmother, my great-grandfather studied for five years in Bukhara and became Janybek's advisor and close friend, whereas my grandmother always spoke about Kurmanjan's arrival at Kakyr. Indeed, you too have authored it.

— *Mamyshev Mirlan*

A PREFACE OF THINGS PAST

According to a number of modern occidental scholars, marauding Scythians eventually settled in present-day Kyrgyzstan. A country truly blessed by natural wonders, alongside an abundance of ecological resources. However, these eternal landscapes always appear to be at odds with the historical processes working upon them. Somehow, the angels themselves seem to be unclear as to whether they want unending, timeless, traditions to thrive atop such soils, or modernity to flourish unabated. In which case, a perpetual tension could be said to exist between Scythians, as well as indigenous Kyrgyz, "then" and "now" on every mountain and pasture of this region.

Briefly looking back, the twelfth century witnessed indigenous Kyrgyz territorial dominion shrinking to the Altai Range and Sayan Mountains as a result of Mongol expansion. Indeed, the burgeoning energies of the Mongol Empire in the thirteenth century even compelled the Kyrgyz to migrate southward in search of autonomy, whereas Issyk Kul Lake contrastingly saw the development of much needed stopovers for traders and other travellers along the Silk Road as they journeyed from the Far East to Europe. Eventually, these innovations noted, the Kyrgyz tribes were overrun in the seventeenth century by the very same Mongol invaders, while the eighteenth century observed political and cultural pressures arise from the Manchurian Qing dynasty in China, not to mention in the nineteenth century by the Uzbek Khanate of Kokand, or for that matter Imperial Russia. Hence, the Kyrgyz tended to embody narratives surrounding inherited authoritarian hierarchies, tribalism and the type of previously unquestioned ideology, which supports a naive patriarchal dominance over other genders amid turbulent advances within their own ethnic ranks. Taken together, they accidentally became a sentient and living laboratory for global evolution.

Each factor above making this genuinely fascinating poem compelling reading. After all, it is the story of an independent, empowered, woman during a period when such things were next to impossible. What is more, a genuine matriarch seeking peace between warring factions at the same time as trying to hold her family together. In which case, I do not have the slightest hesitation in recommending this remarkable epic poetry to Anglophone readers worldwide.

— Rev. Dr. David William Parry FRAS FRAS
London 2021

BUBAISHA ARSTYNBEKOVA
"QUEEN KURMANJAN OF THE MOUNTAINS"

Describing this work as an epic poem does not do it justice! It is more than poetical; it is a history of the traditions and people of Kyrgyzstan. The author paints a detailed picture of the beautiful landscapes of Kyrgyzstan as seen through the eyes of historical figures. She interweaves the traditions that are still held dear to the population today and within the prose explains the relationships between the people and their country. As with any history of battle, bloodshed and conflict, the names of the heroes come thick and fast and it is worth rereading it to get the relationships and chronology in place. This is a marvellous piece that tells the story of an amazing female leader and how, even in her own tragedy, she put the fate of her people first.

— Review by Gareth Stamp

REVIEW TO THE BOOK "QUEEN KURMANJAN OF THE MOUNTAINS" AN EPIC POEM BY BUBAISHA ARSTYNBEKOVA

TThe purpose of the book "Queen Kurmanjan of the Mountains" and its translation is to introduce and show the history of the Kyrgyz people on the one hand and how they were against the soviet power in that period on the other hand, it also shows how powerful, smart, intelligent, brave, wise and motherly the woman who brought up five sons was, raising them to feel real patriotism for their motherland, that woman being the Kyrgyz lady, Kurmanjan Datka. The title "Datka" is a war title that she was awarded for the first time among other Kyrgyz women, for her bravery and loyalty. The content of the poem is quite different from other information, especially when the author depicts Kurmanjan's childhood, you will enjoy reading the tale about the girl from a simple and poor family who was clever, smart and wise from her early years. While translating the book, I felt as if I was among the heroes of the poem. The language of the poem is simple to understand and enjoyable to read. The author depicts the fact that Kurmanjan was the best adviser of her husband and she was known as the "Alai Queen", a title that was given to ger by the Russian general M. D. Skovelev. When Bubaisha describes the main heroes of the poem she also expresses her love for Kurmanjan, describing and comparing her with the stars in the sky. The author also showed all the customs and traditions of the Kyrgyz nation in a poetic way, customs that were very important in Kurmanjan's life.

B. Arstynbekova describes not only a beautiful and wise lady but also a strong fighter, a hero who fights for the freedom of the nation as well as for her own freedom, all written in a very high poetic style. While reading the poem you can't help but admire the beauty of Kyrgyz nature. One of the most important moments is Kurmanjan's meeting with Alymbek Datka, and it was best described in these pages, even among any other creations and sources that exist. Bubaisha depicted her as the best diplomat among the Kyrgyz people.

The main idea of the poem was the freedom and establishment of the peaceful life among the Kyrgyz nation that Alymbek sought after. As an instrumental politician in the increasingly decrepit Kokand khanate, Alymbek was murdered during a palace coup in 1862 and his widow Kurmanjan was recognized by the khans of Bukhara and Kokand as ruler of the Alai and was given the title of "Datka".

At last, I would like to say to the readers that the author wanted to tell a very beautiful story, about the love of the two great personalities of the Kyrgyz nation like Alymbek and Kurmanjan and its beautiful depiction. I hope that by reading this poem the peoples of the world will know all about the beautiful, wise, and intelligent lady known as Kurmanjan, who fought for the freedom of her nation, sacrificing everything in her life for the sake of the welfare of her people.

— Karaeva Zina. Doctor of philology,
Professor of the International University of Kyrgyzstan.
translator of this great poetry about " Kurmanjan Datka"

QUEEN KURMANJAN OF THE MOUNTAINS

The rise to power and legendary diplomacy of Kyrgyzstan's first female 'Datka' and Central Asia's first stateswoman, are revered throughout her country, with Kurmanjan's life and achievements explored in film, literature and poetry. Hailed as 'Mother' of the Kyrgyz nation, she is honoured by monuments in Bishkek and Osh and her image, from her only photograph taken when she was 96, adorns the 50 som banknote.

Kurmanjan Datka (1811- 1907) operated in fairly recent times but because Kyrgyzstan was long hidden behind the Iron Curtain, it is only now that her story, like those of the nation's ancient heroes and integral to the nation's rich heritage, are reaching the Western world.

Bubaisha Arstynbekova's poem is an empathetic and emotionally colourful account of the journey and legacy of history's most resilient women. Supported by liberal-minded parents and the love of a man who invested her with power, Kurmanjan never cowed from controversy, from fleeing an unhappy arranged marriage and breaking the taboo of divorce, to continuing her late husband's battle for national unity and ultimately, sacrificing her own son in a quest for her peoples' peace.

The epic poem, perhaps an unusual format for a tale set in the 19th century, adheres to a long tradition which not only provided gravitas to the stories being told, but ensured that they were never forgotten. Following tradition, it also gives scope for the integration of indigenous songs, verse and proverbs; lyrical descriptions of the landscape and characters' emotions; vivid and punchy accounts of battles, and details of local customs.

In this, Bubaisha Arstynbekova excels. From the very first stanza, the reader is transported to a foreign land and quickly immersed in a wealth of fascinating and alien customs and politics. A master of her craft, she is able to outline complex political scenarios in very few words and despite the obvious cultural differences, provides well-rounded characters to whom we can all relate.

Queen Kurmanjan of the Mountains is a gripping saga which will undoubtedly enthral English readers and once gripped, encourage further exploration of Kyrgyzstan's rich and varied heritage.

— *Laura Hamilton, Editor*

www.ingramcontent.com/pod-product-compliance
Lightning Source LLC
Chambersburg PA
CBHW030559310726
48979CB00003B/503

* 9 7 8 1 9 1 3 3 5 6 3 2 3 *